D0513496

Creating
a
HOME

Creating a HOME

RACHEL LEWIS

Colour Library Direct

CLD 21133
This edition published in 1998 for
Colour Library Direct
Godalming Business Centre
Woolsack Way
Godalming
Surrey GU7 1XW

© Parragon 1997

All rights reserved. No part of this publication may be reproduced, stored in a retrieval system, or transmitted in any way or by any means, electronic, mechanical, photocopying, recording or otherwise, without the prior permission of the copyright holder.

ISBN 1-85833-933-2

Designed, produced and packaged by
Touchstone
Old Chapel Studio
Plain Road
Marden
Tonbridge
Kent TN12 9LS

Picture research by Emily Hedges

Printed in Italy

Contents

Starting Out

▽ If you like to spend a lot of time in the kitchen, the styling will be important to you. This wooden, rustic-style arrangement is both attractive and practical.

Whether you are moving into a new home or just want to give your existing rooms a facelift, designing the decor is one of the most exciting parts of creating your home.

Think first of all about the order in which the rooms will be decorated. Do you have the luxury of restyling before moving in or will you have to do one room at a time while living in the other areas? Do you know what styles appeal or will you need to do some research first?

Research can be great fun – take time to leaf through books and magazines on interior decorating, go to large or specialist stores and wander around the home departments, looking at fabric, light fittings, door handles, paint charts, rugs, carpets and the furniture ranges. Collect swatches for later reference and take time to get a general impression of what you like best for each particular room.

Cost need not be prohibitive. There are all sorts of handy hints and decorating ideas explained in this book which will allow you to create wonderful rooms within your budget. Soon you too will have a stunning, stylish home, whatever your preferred decorative scheme, be it bold and bright, cool and classic, traditional and refined – or simply a collection of what you like best.

△ A bright, fresh bedroom scheme is easily created using a bold combination of colour co-ordinated furnishing fabrics, bedlinen and wallpapers.

△ A country-style look is achieved through a combination of natural materials and pretty fabrics.

▷ If you do not have the time or money for a complete refit, the bathroom can be a good place to start. Fresh paintwork and a change of fittings can give a new lease of life to a tired room.

Warm Tones

▽ In this bright and airy room, the naturally warm tones of the wood floor and matching furniture are complemented by the orange, red and yellow colours in the fabrics used in the soft furnishings.

You can apply colour to almost any part of a room, in the soft furnishings and upholstery, on painted furniture, on the woodwork and on the floors; it can also appear on the walls, ceiling and at the windows. Pictures on the walls and accessories and ornaments all add colour to a room.

You will need to think judiciously about the colours you use in your creative styling. First of all, consider the effect you would like the room to have on mood and impression of space. Dark colours bring the walls inward for a comfortable, welcoming feel and so may be most suitable for rooms that are very large. Remember to try a sample patch of paint in the room to check that it is the right shade – a very dark colour may turn out to be overpowering and you may prefer a lighter shade.

Do you prefer a single, strong splash of colour, say on a sofa or in a curtain treatment, carefully balanced against contrasting walls? Or do you enjoy the uplifting mix-and-match effect of placing different fabrics and paint shades

△ An excellent example of a warm colour set in perfect contrast against a bright, acidic shade. Here the pistachio green offsets the rich brick orange on both the wall and the armchair.

◁ The use of darker, warm shades in a carpet or other floor covering can be very pleasing. Not only will this tartan carpet hide the dirt well, but it becomes a focal feature of the room, especially when contrasted with pale furniture and walls. The tartan theme is continued in the throw on the sofa.

together from a similar or contrasting colour range? Collect lots of pictures, fabric and flooring samples and paint charts, and experiment in miniature before committing yourself to a scheme. Look around for inspiration, and do not be afraid to experiment – even the most unusual warm colour combinations can work well.

△ Dark to light: clever use of a warm colour on one wall leading to an expanse of white beyond.

COOL SHADES

∇ Pretty pastel colours are used together to give a sense of space and light in this dining area. The same shades of yellow and blue are found in the contrasting patterns of the table cloth, wallpaper and curtain divider.

While rich, dark colours are often used in a decorative scheme to bring a sense of closeness and warmth to a room, light, pale colours can be applied to achieve a sense of airiness and space. If your room is very small or does not receive much light, painting or papering the walls in a pale shade may make the area seem brighter and larger.

As with any colour scheme, test your chosen shade as a patch sample before going ahead with decorating the whole room. If you have decided on a wallpaper, hang a large swatch in the room and live with it for a few days while you make absolutely sure that it is the right choice. Even the palest of colours can affect a room: a tinted white, for example, may appear too grey under the artificial lights used in the evening, or an apparently soothing pale green can seem a little too acidic over a large area.

Cool colours are easy to combine, particularly in colours that, when used in dense concentrations, would form contrasts. Pale blues, greens and yellows can all be combined with ease, each shade offsetting the other. These colours work very well together in a home just as they do in the garden. Pale pinks and creams with a touch of blue or yellow also form pretty decorative schemes. In a combined scheme each colour can be used in varying amounts, perhaps with one shade forming the basis of the design and the others providing touches of contrast.

Another form of contrast can be created when decorating with cool or pale shades which is quite different from the use of conbined pastels. Paint the room a single cool colour, such as white, cream or pale yellow. Choose furniture in the same shade. Then, selecting styles and shapes that you like, place a few brightly coloured accessories around the room to break up the pale expanse, being careful to avoid a cluttered effect.

△ Cool greens and creams used in a restful scheme. The chair echoes the colour of the upper wall while the border forms a unifying strip.

◁ Sea green and blue produce a calm effect in this marine-theme bathroom, with accessories to match.

Practicalities

When choosing cool colours, bear in mind the use of the room and the furniture. If you have young children, consider using washable wallpapers and paints, and, in the sitting room, selecting a sofa with removable, machine washable covers. Paler colours have a tendency to show the dirt more than darker colours or designs without patterns.

◁ Cool colours need not always be pale. This sitting room is decorated in varying shades of blue, with a recurring leaf motif in white on the walls and curtain fabric which lifts the overall scheme.

Neutrals

▽ This peaceful bedroom scheme combines several neutral colours in the soft furnishings chosen. These colours complement the natural materials in the room such as the metal of the bed frame, the wood floor and the rug.

Decorating with neutrals is very satisfying because the design scheme always looks elegant and sophisticated. Neutral colours are those that blend in with any colour scheme, and one way of identifying them is to think of colours that occur in nature. Neutrals include a wide range of shades and tones of whites, creams, beiges, taupes, greys and pale browns. They can be combined with other, stronger colours in a decorative scheme, often forming an unobtrusive backdrop to the overall design.

This is not to say that neutrals must always play second fiddle in a room – far from it. For instant sophistication, plan your room around a single neutral colour, or a combination of several, such as shades of cream and ivory, for instance. The colour scheme can encompass the walls, floor, ceiling and furniture, even the accessories. If you wish to add a splash of colour, plants or dishes in terracotta or sandstone blend in beautifully, as do flowers in pale yellow or white in glass or stoneware vases.

If you are using more than one neutral colour, as with any colour scheme, arrange samples and swatches first just to check that the overall effect is what you are hoping for. If the design looks a little drab, add a shade that is lighter or darker – perhaps only as an accessory – and consider the difference that this makes.

One other pleasure in using neutrals is that of being able to experiment with different textures within the same colour range. Using neutrals alone emphasizes the patterns and weaves in fabric or the deliberate inconsistencies in a wall, for example. If you enjoy the look of natural materials then this is a perfect way of combining several different pieces of wood, natural fabrics and stone. On the other hand, for the modernist, a neutral scheme can also make the most of sleek plastic and metal pieces.

Examples of Neutrals

Three different types of neutrals: the sitting room (top) is based on a mixture of taupes and ivory shades; the reading corner (centre) is a warm combination of cream and wood with a dash of colour in the red border, while the bedroom (bottom) uses cool, clear white.

△ An exciting African feel is achieved in this sitting room with a background of contrasting patterned wallpapers in rust and cream. The use of wooden furniture and accessories in the decorative plan helps to continue the richness of this neutral scheme.

Styling Your Home

▽ This informal sitting room has a mixture of styles within it, including Native American and Folk Art, yet they work well together to form a comfortable, homely look.

Settling on a style for your home takes some confidence, a little daring and a spirit of adventure. Look around you at friends' homes and at arrangements in shops and magazines and gradually decide on what you like to have around you. Do not be put off by one person making negative comments about your choices – taste is completely individual and no two households are ever exactly alike.

You may decide on a unifying style for all the rooms in your home, or you may prefer to select a different theme for

◁ A more formal style of sitting room is produced using a traditional armchair and fireplace as well as using the original panelling of the house as a backdrop. An unexpectedly modern touch, which enlivens the overall look of the room, is the bright red colour used on the panelling. This lifts the scheme and gives the room a warm and contemporary appearance.

▽ This bright and cheerful child's room has been created using a mixture of strong primary colours in co-ordinating fabric and wallpaper designs. The toy motif border serves as a decorative strip that unifies the wall scheme, while the clever addition of contrasting dots on the door panels emphasizes the matching dots on the lower portion of the walls.

each area; a country kitchen, a marine-style bathroom and a comfortable but traditional sitting or living room. There is no reason why each room should be the same. After all, in a house with children, each child's room will become as individual as they are – especially as they grow older – so why not impose your own taste and style on a couple of the rooms too?

If you have been in your current home for some time, the years will have gone by and fashions and practical needs may have changed. Be prepared to step back from your original decor and decide on something new. This may be nerve-wracking as you embark on altering what have been your most familiar surroundings for some time, but it will be worth it when admiring friends and family come to have a look and the compliments flow thick and fast.

Paint Effects

△ Decorative effects on accessories work well. This pottery vase has been speckled in two similar colours.

If you are a keen painter or decorating enthusiast then paint effects are definitely for you. You can take direct inspiration from an example you have seen, or one that you will find in the later pages of this book, or you can experiment with variations on texture and colour. If you are nervous about committing your first efforts to the wall or floor or favourite item of furniture, work on a piece of scrap wood or on an area of wall which you can paint over if the effect is not as desired.

Floors as well as walls take paint effects very well. The range is vast, and the variations and colours limitless. The effects particularly suited to floor areas are colourwashing or painting of wooden boards, perhaps with a stamped or stencilled design on top. Alternatively you can add handpainted details to the background colours. Marbling and wood graining are very effective, but are perhaps best suited to walls unless you are prepared to apply several coats of tough, protective varnish. Painted canvas floorcloths also allow you to experiment with decorative effects, without painting directly onto the floor itself. If you do not have suitable wooden boards on your floor, lay down good-quality hardboard and paint this instead.

△ Stippling creates a subtle effect if, as here, two shades from the same range of colours are used.

▷ These dining room walls have been lightly colourwashed and then given the extra effect of handpainted panel frames, created by a thick border within two thin lines.

Paint effects work extremely well on walls, which is their better known application. Try sponging, stippling or ragging to achieve a broken colour effect, perhaps using two shades of the same colour. Marbling and wood graining take time but the final result is very rewarding, being elegant and refined. Colourwashing one colour over another, often in striking contrast to the first, can create some marvellous effects. Liming and staining of wood, which works well on floor boards, can look beautiful; if you do not have wood on the walls you can fit panelling or tongue and groove strips up to dado-rail height. Do not forget the art of trompe l'oeil painting, where you give an impression of a scene or objects through canny imitation. Murals too allow free reign to the imagination, and are particularly suitable for children's rooms and stairwells.

STAMPING: This technique involves using a shaped pad to apply (or remove) paint to form a decorative effect. The pad is dipped into a shallow layer of paint, applied evenly to the surface and then removed. The pattern can be repeated as you like.

△ Dragging is a popular technique that imitates plain wood grain. The use of unusual colours makes the decorative element more striking.

△ A bolder effect is achieved by using a wood graining technique. Here a rough grain, such as that found in pine, is produced yet in a non-wood colour.

△ Colourwashing need not be restrained: this bathroom wall has been decorated in bold strokes to create a strong sense of movement and warmth.

The Essentials

Before you begin to restyle your home, if you plan on doing some or all of the decorating yourself gather together a basic set of tools and collect some essential pieces of equipment. First and foremost, you will need a number of large dustsheets to protect floors and furniture from paint and plaster splashes. Old cotton bed sheets are fine, and you may want to invest in a couple of large polythene or plastic sheets from the local home improvement store. Often friends and neighbours have a collection of dustsheets that they are only too happy to lend so do not be afraid to ask around.

A certain amount of equipment can be hired from your local tool hire company. This avoids purchasing items that you are not likely to use frequently. Among the most useful items to hire may be a steam wallpaper stripper and an electric floor sander (essential for preparing floorboards for a paint effect). Remember to hire goggles and mask at the same time.

The basics

A selection of decorator's brushes in different sizes, some pails for mixing paint and plaster, a spatula and of course some sticks for mixing are essential, as are lint-free rags for wiping brushes and for removing any little splashes of paint. A papering table on trestles, a large bucket for mixing wallpaper paste and a wallpaper pasting brush are important if you will be papering your walls; do not forget a pair of long-bladed scissors and a craft knife for trimming the ends of the sheets.

▽ Essential painting equipment: brushes and rollers in different sizes, a paint tray and a paint bucket.

△ Place contrasting borders and fabrics together in the room to check that they form the desired effect

As you decide on what improvements you would like to make, you will have a clearer picture of the equipment you need. Do not feel that you have to spend a great deal right at the beginning – see what you need and buy everything but the basics as you progress with the job, purchasing what you need for each room before you start on that particular area.

△ Choose from the vast range of borders and trimmings.

▽ Use paint pads for covering large areas of wall and blow lamps and scrapers for paint removal.

Making An Entrance

The hallway of your home is the first thing you and your guests will see, so you will want it to be both welcoming and in the style of the rest of your decor. Following a few simple guidelines will allow you to have an entranceway you can be proud of and which is as practical as possible.

First of all, consider your colour scheme. If the hallway tends to lack natural light and is quite small, you may want to choose light-coloured wall coverings or paint to make it seem airier. If the ceiling is high and the space feels cold and slightly intimidating, a warm, dark colour such as burnt sienna or terracotta can help transform the area into a comforting, all-embracing entranceway.

△ A stunning geometric arrangement of Victorian-style floor tiles always makes an impact in an entrance hall; this type of tile is very hardwearing.

Safety

Safety is of great importance on stairs and landings. Make sure that the stair covering is non-slip and that you do not place any small rugs at the top of the staircase or on a polished floor. Remember to allow for adequate lighting in all parts of the stairwell, especially if it passes around a corner, and fit light switches at both the bottom and top of the stairs.

Practical considerations are important in the hallway and stairwell. The hallway and stairs will be the most frequently used part of your home, and will receive a lot of wear and tear, especially if you have children or pets or

live in the countryside. Choose long-lasting, washable wall coverings, such as vinyl paints which can be wiped clean or even scrubbed gently.

If you choose a paint technique for hallway walls, apply at least two coats of varnish to protect the surface. Your choice of floor covering needs to be hardwearing and easy to clean to withstand the constant passage of feet, often, perhaps, covered in mud. The floor should also be nonslip, particularly on the stairs, and a sturdy, removeable mat just inside the front door will bear the brunt of most of the dirt.

△ This hallway uses a neutral scheme of cream and beige, with the additional detail of a contrasting carpet border.

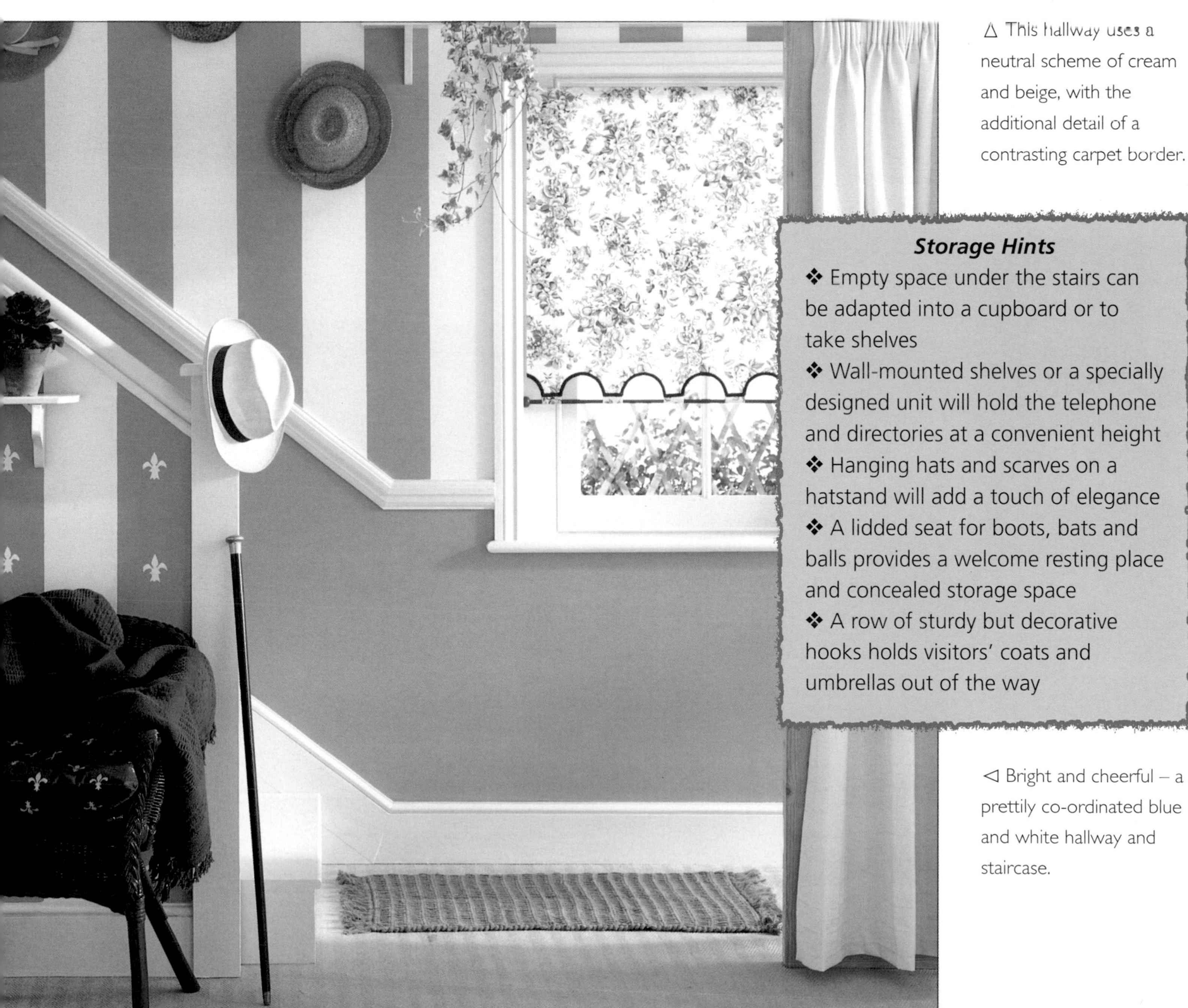

Storage Hints

❖ Empty space under the stairs can be adapted into a cupboard or to take shelves

❖ Wall-mounted shelves or a specially designed unit will hold the telephone and directories at a convenient height

❖ Hanging hats and scarves on a hatstand will add a touch of elegance

❖ A lidded seat for boots, bats and balls provides a welcome resting place and concealed storage space

❖ A row of sturdy but decorative hooks holds visitors' coats and umbrellas out of the way

◁ Bright and cheerful – a prettily co-ordinated blue and white hallway and staircase.

Traditional Taste

△ A traditional curtain and border treatment.

▽ The border and curtains pick up the red of the sofa upholstery.

The sitting room is where you will receive your visitors and relax at the end of the day. It is the room where you can really allow your decorative scheme to reflect your personal taste. The traditional style of decor is ideally suited

▷ Beautifully draped pelmets and curtains frame the double windows in this classic sitting room. The same fabric is used on the seats and is complemented by the colours in the rug and wall-hung tapestry.

to a sitting room – it is calm, uncluttered and refined, but need not be reserved solely for the wealthiest of homes.

An eye for colour and classic design will serve you well and you will find that most stores have beautiful, traditional lines.

A long sweep of fabric made up into curtains or drapes, often with decorative poles and finials and co-ordinating or contrasting tiebacks, immediately adds height and elegance to a room, especially when the fabric design is chosen to match or cleverly offset the choice of soft furnishings. Cushions, upholstered stools and a lounge suite of sofa and armchairs can all be co-ordinated to present an attractive ensemble. The walls can be decorated using plain paint, a more elaborate paint effect such as a small-scale stencil, or covered in a traditional-style wallpaper, perhaps with the addition of a border that picks out a colour or motif in the fabric design.

Focal Point

If you are lucky enough to have an original fireplace, or decide to put one into the sitting room, this will become a focal point for your decorative scheme. A luxurious-looking rug and a hearth set of coal bucket and tongs will quickly provide a homely touch.

▽ The huge fireplace has been retained in this comfortable sitting room, its brick interior and wood surround forming an effective contrast to the mint-green walls. The accessories and ornaments all fit in well with the traditional feel.

Modern Moods

▽ Cool lines reflect the cool colours of this sleek room. The accessories and furniture have the same clean lines as seen in the fireplace surround, the colour of which is picked up almost exactly in the sofa fabric.

If you prefer sleeker lines or the bursts of colour in contemporary fabrics, a modern sitting room is for you. This look is easier to achieve if you select your accessories carefully, aiming for a minimalist or co-ordinated look, with a few decorative touches provided by pottery vases, unusual bowls and modern lamps or candlesticks.

The choice of colour is also important; you may like the 'naturals' ranges that co-ordinate so effortlessly, bringing together unbleached cotton upholstery fabrics, soft cotton voiles to create a muted light at the window, and sisal or coir matting on the floor. Alternatively, try offsetting splashes of colour in the form of cushions and

The Sleek Look

Choose ornaments for the modern room with care. Sleek lines, evocative of the best of twentieth-century design, can be found in contemporary lamps, vases, bowls and bookcases.

throws on pale sofas and the occasional, metal-framed picture set against white or muted walls. Mix and match wood and stone (such as sand- and soapstone or marble) with glass, ceramics, wicker, hessian and the new linens, rich with texture and light.

Modern rooms allow you to choose modern furniture – whether it is from a range inspired by a famous 'retro' designer or a completely new piece that particularly catches your eye. Or combine interesting styles from different eras. Have fun experimenting with shapes and textures – there are no rules and the style will be entirely your own.

△ Unusual colour combinations can work well in modern rooms. Here the green of the fireplace and dado rail contrasts with the two different wall tones.

△ Natural materials in a variety of neutral tones are placed together in this sitting room to achieve a very relaxing effect.

Sponging

The paint technique of sponging is one of the easiest to pick up. You do not need specialist equipment and with only a little experimenting you are ready to begin. Sponging involves applying paint to walls (or furniture, even) using a sponge and a thin layer of paint. It is best to use a natural sponge rather than a man-made one because the pattern of the holes is less regular.

Sponging can be done using one or more colours of paint on top of a base

A Good Disguise

Sponging is a useful technique for applying to uneven wall surfaces. It disguises any bumps, cracks or lumps with the mottled imprint of the sponge and can also camouflage textured wallpaper such as woodchip paper. As a technique it can be applied to almost any surface.

▷ A special feature has been made of the sponging in this sitting room. Cream-painted walls have been divided into panels and pink sponging applied inside the panelled area. The pink chosen for the sponging matches the colour of the sofa, rug and picture mounts.

coat. Make sure that this base coat is completely dry before you start to sponge. The effect produced depends on the colours you choose and the pressure with which you apply them on the sponge. Pressing lightly produces a subtle effect while heavy pressure forms a more dramatic pattern.

Always experiment before starting to apply paint to the walls. Try sponging at different pressures on a piece of paper until you achieve the required effect.

You will need:

- ❖ Rubber gloves
- ❖ Natural sponge
- ❖ Cold water
- ❖ Matt emulsion paint
- ❖ Paint tray
- ❖ Lint-free cotton rag

◁ Step 1: Moisten the sponge until it is damp all over. Pour some matt emulsion paint into the paint tray. Dip the sponge into the paint and dab off any excess onto the rag to make sure that the sponge is not overloaded with paint.

◁ Step 2: Working steadily but without rushing, make sponge marks at random over the wall, working on a fairly small area at a time. Try to space the paint marks equally. Recharge the sponge as necessary.

◁ Step 3: Keep dipping the sponge into the paint so that the pattern does not become too faint. When you have finished the first layer of sponging, fill in the gaps between marks with a second layer for a more mottled effect.

Cheap Chic

It is entirely possible to create a stunning sitting room at very little expense and with a great deal of style. Old furniture can be given a new lease of life with some bright cushions or fashionable throws, the windows can be dressed in co-ordinating blinds and curtains while the walls can also be decorated in matching hues. Even the floors can be given a new lease of life; rugs laid over worn or shabby carpets, scrubbed and varnished wooden boards and painted and stencilled hardboard sheeting all give a bright, chic look to the room.

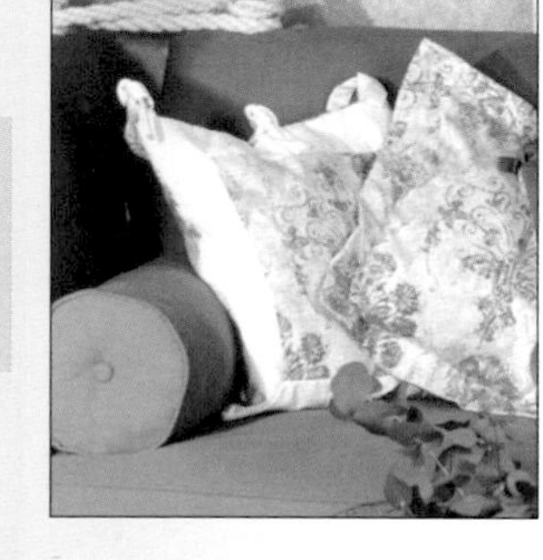

△ Inexpensive and easy steps towards creating a new look – add a cheap curtain pole for a traditional touch (top) and hang curtains using fabric loops (centre); make up co-ordinating cushions from offcuts of the curtain fabric.

▷ A bright, cheerful country look achieved at very little cost – curtains form a dividing wall and cut down on draughts.

If you can only afford one new piece of furniture, it will probably be the sofa so try to make this the centrepiece of the room, decorating it with attractive cushions and tying the rest of the decor into the colour of the upholstery. After all, you will want to make the most of your new and stylish acquisition.

Old wooden or melamine furniture can be spruced up very quickly with a coat of paint or some stencilled motifs. Alternatively, try one of the many paint effects, from woodgraining and marbling to colourwashing and antiquing. If the effect is successful on a small piece of furniture, consider applying it around the room, perhaps in more muted colours, on the skirting board or doors, or even on a suitable lampshade.

▷ Inexpensive rush matting and inventive use of accessories together with the rich yellow mottled ragged walls make this room especially chic.

△ Plain white walls and floor provide the perfect background for the simple blue and white sofa and armchair arrangement. Sophisticated simplicity is easy to achieve.

Small touches for a new look

❖ Replace old doorhandles with new, catchy models, perhaps in ceramic or crystal

❖ Catch back curtains with colourful braids, or use remnants of fabric to make tiebacks with pretty tassels

❖ Brighten up plain walls with a decorative border at ceiling or dado-rail height

❖ Add plants in bright pots for an immediate facelift

Co-ordinated Hues

You can have great fun deciding on a colour-co-ordinated room scheme. First of all choose a colour that appeals to you and create a sample board around the different shades of this colour. To make a sample board, collect pictures of rooms or pieces of furniture from magazines and catalogues and stick them onto a large sheet of paper together with paint chart samples, swatches or fabric and pieces of wallpaper, anything in fact that appeals.

Do not be afraid to mix and match patterns and textures, as long as you stick to the same colour range or combination of colours. If the look as a whole risks becoming overpowering, add a plain colour in a pale tone or co-

ordinating neutral shade and think of using this as a background shade to break up the overall effect.

When you are happy with the style, put it into practice. Look around shops and showrooms and choose your wall and floor colours and furniture to match. You will be surprised at the different patterns and textures that can be placed together in a single room as long as they fit into the overall colour scheme.

Do not be afraid to mix florals with checks or stripes, stencilled motifs with patterned rugs, and plain walls with extravagant swirls of colour in the fabric designs. You can be as daring as you like within the range of your chosen colour or colours.

◁ This room presents an appearance of peace and elegance. It is decorated using shades of grey-blue, with touches of deep pink in the fabric motif and a white carpet and fireplace to ensure that the effect is not too dark.

▷ Quite the opposite impression is created here: this bright sitting room is classical without appearing too formal. The main colour of apricot is beautifully co-ordinated with red and green tones in the fabrics and wall coverings.

Colour Inspiration

If you are not starting entirely from scratch in the design of your room, for instance if you already possess some furniture or cannot change the colour of the carpet, use these as the starting point for your scheme. If they are a very pale or neutral colour use this to offset the main colour scheme, preventing it from becoming too powerful. If you are happy with the colour of your sofa, say, then match the rest of the room to this, choosing rugs, curtains, cushions and accessories to co-ordinate. What was once your ordinary sofa will suddenly be given a new lease of life in the redesigned colour scheme. If all else fails and it is imperative that you change the colour of the sofa, throw a cover in the colour of your choice over it and pretend that you are starting afresh!

DRAGGING

Dragging is the technique used to produce a "grained" effect in paint, and is sometimes used to imitate wood grain. The effect can be used on walls but is often more suitable for woodwork such as on panels or skirting boards. Dragging is usually carried out on top of a white or plain base coat of eggshell paint which has a slightly glossy surface that prevents the dragging coat from being absorbed. This is important because the dragging coat of paint is

You will need:
- ❖ Transparent oil glaze
- ❖ Artist's oil paint
- ❖ White spirit (if necessary)
- ❖ Mixing pot
- ❖ Paint tray
- ❖ Paint roller
- ❖ Wide, coarse-bristled paint brush
- ❖ Lint-free cotton rag
- ❖ Brush for applying varnish
- ❖ Clear matt polyurethane varnish

▷ This room uses a clever combination of paint techniques – the walls have been painted a plain colour above the dado rail and have been ragged beneath the rail. The cupboard door panels have been dragged in a matching colour for a perfectly co-ordinated decorative scheme.

partially removed by the technique and so needs to sit on the surface of the base coat. When the technique is complete, the paint adheres to the base coat in the normal way. The base coat should be dry before you begin dragging.

Dragging uses transparent oil glaze mixed with artist's oil paint to produce the required colour. If the paint seems too thick it can be thinned with white spirit. Remember to experiment on scrap paper until you are happy with the colour.

△ Step 1: Having mixed the coloured glaze, apply it to the area to be decorated using a paint roller.

△ Step 2: Using the wide paint brush, drag the bristles down through the paint in long, steady strokes.

△ Step 3: Remove the paint that collects on the brush using a lint-free cotton rag to prevent ugly streaks.

△ Step 4: The effect should be that of continuous lines. When the paint is dry, apply a coat of clear varnish.

DINING SMALL

▽ Despite the lack of space, this dining room has been given a bright and sunny look by the use of lively colours in the window treatment and chair cushion fabric. The round table allows for varying numbers of diners.

Bright colours and careful choice of furniture will make a small dining room more adaptable both for daytime and evening use. Storage will be an important factor, allowing you to keep cutlery, table linens and crockery in the room so that you are not always carrying items back and forth from the kitchen. The most useful item of furniture for a dining room is probably a dresser or sideboard, with a combination of cupboards and drawers, and, on a dresser, the chance to display your favourite dishes or glassware on the shelves, adding a practical but decorative touch to the room.

The most important piece of furniture in a small dining room is the table. It will need to be large enough to seat everyone in the household, as well as any visiting relatives and friends. If you have children, it may well be used for other activities besides eating; children's painting and modelling sessions, birthday parties and work brought home from the office may all have their turn in the room. For this reason, you may want to choose an expandable or folding table to make the most of the limited space available. A folding table can be pushed against a wall when not in use.

If the room is fairly narrow, you may want to consider using a hardwearing, washable wallpaper, at least up to dado-

Space-saving tips

❖ Store the crockery and table linen in the kitchen or in an understairs cupboard if you do not have the storage space in the dining room itself

❖ Make the most of the tight space to create an intimate atmosphere for dinner parties: subdued lighting and candles are perfect, especially as the dim light conceals the size of the room

rail height. This means that any scrapes from chair backs or smudges from children's hands can be cleaned or concealed against a dark patterned design. If you prefer to use paint, select a washable vinyl type so that marks can easily be wiped off.

△ This pretty dining room has been given a cottage feel, which is not at odds with its intimate size. The unified decor mixes and matches the designs in the wall coverings with the blind, tablecloth and napkins and director's chair. Both this chair and the table can be folded away if the room needs to be used for another purpose, making the most of the space.

△ Details are important in a small room, and accessories can offer practical storage space as well as decorative value.

Dining In Style

An elegant dining room will be used primarily – if not solely – for entertaining and formal meals. The decorative scheme should reflect this, and as well as being refined should be welcoming and stylish. A well-matched colour scheme incorporating the walls, floors, table linen and dining furniture will form the essence of the room's style, producing the perfect background for delightful accessories and tableware.

Wallpaper and paint colours can be used together, perhaps keeping one wall plainer than the others and standing a dresser or glass-fronted cabinet in front of it. The plain wall colour can also act as a wonderful backdrop to framed paintings or prints, which can be chosen to highlight some of the colours used in the overall decorative scheme. For a classical touch, panelling can look very elegant, while wallpaper up to the level of a dado rail followed by paint or a paint technique above can add extra visual interest.

It is on the dining table that you can allow your creative senses free reign; if you enjoy experimenting with table settings, make up a collection of swatches of coloured paper napkins, napkin rings in different designs, candles and candelabra or candle holders, miniature flower vases and place cards. Buy a selection of table cloths in different colours or patterns, and have fun co-ordinating each table setting with the colours of the room.

△ The classical elegance of this room is achieved by the use of a traditional floral design in the co-ordinating fabrics and wallpaper, which continues above the dado rail. The stylish effect is enhanced by the double folding doors.

△ The rich colours of this design scheme – deep crimson and muted apple green – work well with the dark wood furniture and the large candelabra.

▷ For a Renaissance look, curtain off the dining area with generously fringed drapes and cord tiebacks. Choose furniture and lighting to match.

Lighting

An atmospheric room requires effective lighting, and this is particularly true of the dining room where you and your guests will linger for several hours. Candles on the table will create a comfortable, informal scene, while lights artfully placed within uplighting sconces around the room will produce a subtle, warm effect, allowing you to serve food and wine without disturbing the ambience.

WALLPAPERING

Hanging wallpaper is a quick way to make a home look elegant and well decorated. There are many different types of designs to suit all budgets and tastes, from textured finishes, anaglypta patterns, florals, geometrics, imitation paint effects and even those that contain small pieces of gold leaf. Matching borders are available in many ranges.

Ready-pasted wallpapers are also available, and can be useful when space and time are limited.

△ Step 1: Measure and mark the drop required, allowing 1 in (2.5 cm) extra on both the top and bottom of each piece.

△ Step 2: Cut the lengths of wallpaper at the marks. Give each drop a number and mark which end is the top.

△ Step 3: Mix the wallpaper paste and brush onto the wrong side of the first drop, starting at the middle and working to the edge.

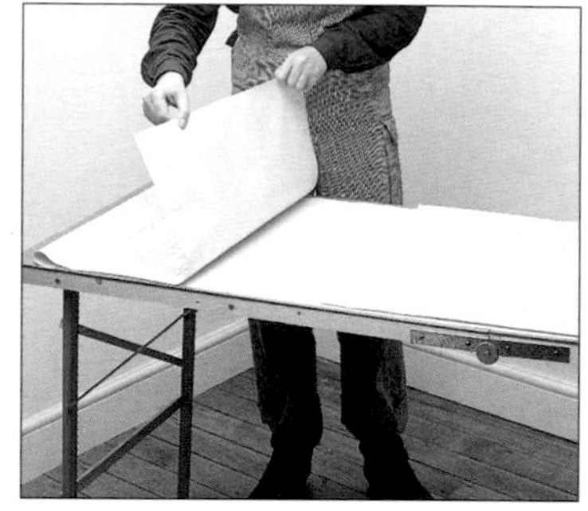

△ Step 4: Fold each end to the middle and to the middle again, Leave the paper to absorb the paste, and paste all the drops.

△ Step 5: Unfold the first piece at the top and position so that it overlaps both the corner and the ceiling by 1 in (2.5 cm).

△ Step 6: Unfold the rest of the drop. Starting from the top, smooth out any air bubbles using the wallpaper brush.

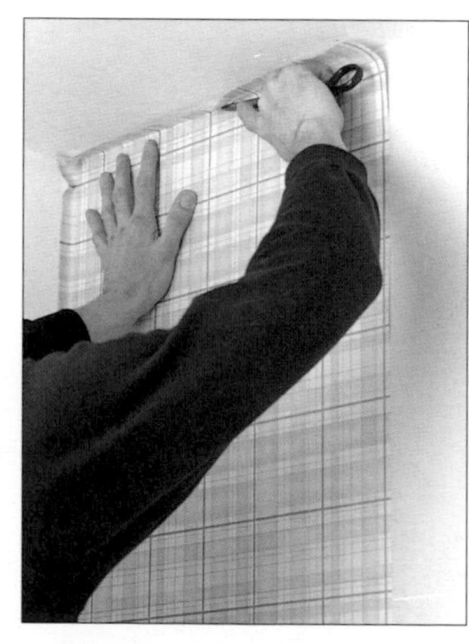

△ Step 7: Mark the ceiling join using the back of the scissor blades. Follow the contours of the join. Trim above the mark.

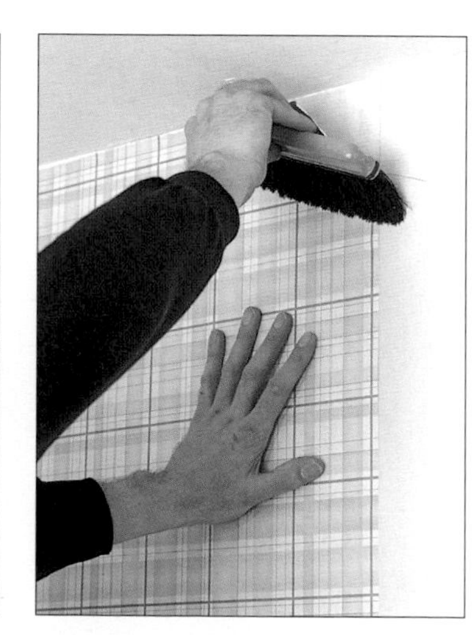

△ Step 8: Brush the trimmed edge into place. Repeat at the skirting board. Continue hanging drops working from left to right.

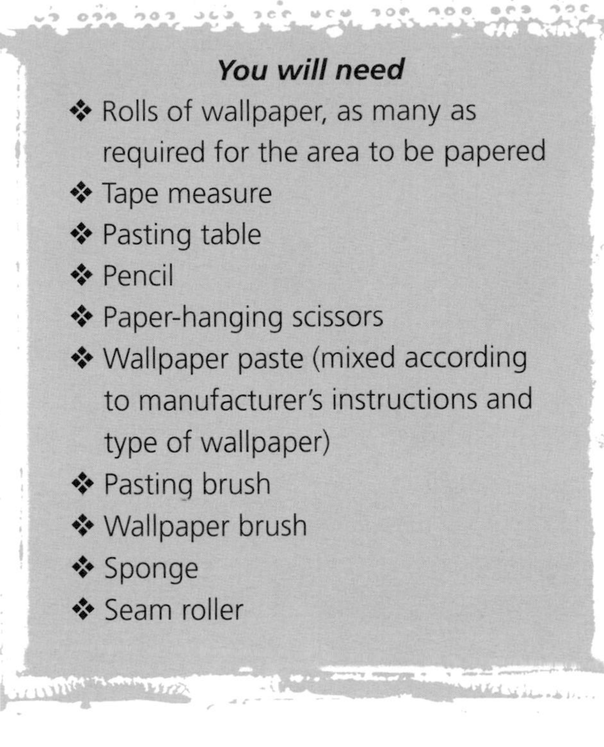

You will need

- ❖ Rolls of wallpaper, as many as required for the area to be papered
- ❖ Tape measure
- ❖ Pasting table
- ❖ Pencil
- ❖ Paper-hanging scissors
- ❖ Wallpaper paste (mixed according to manufacturer's instructions and type of wallpaper)
- ❖ Pasting brush
- ❖ Wallpaper brush
- ❖ Sponge
- ❖ Seam roller

When buying wallpaper always check that all the rolls have the same batch number to ensure that the colours match. Your local home improvement store or specialist supplier will be able to help you calculate how many rolls to buy, and advise you on whether you need a little extra to match a pattern.

△ Many wallpaper designs are available as part of a co-ordinating range. This design features a matching border with a larger version of the motifs.

◁ To use ready-pasted wallpaper, soak in water and then hang, smoothing with a sponge.

▷ To ensure the seams are smooth, roll with a seam roller, wiping away excess adhesive.

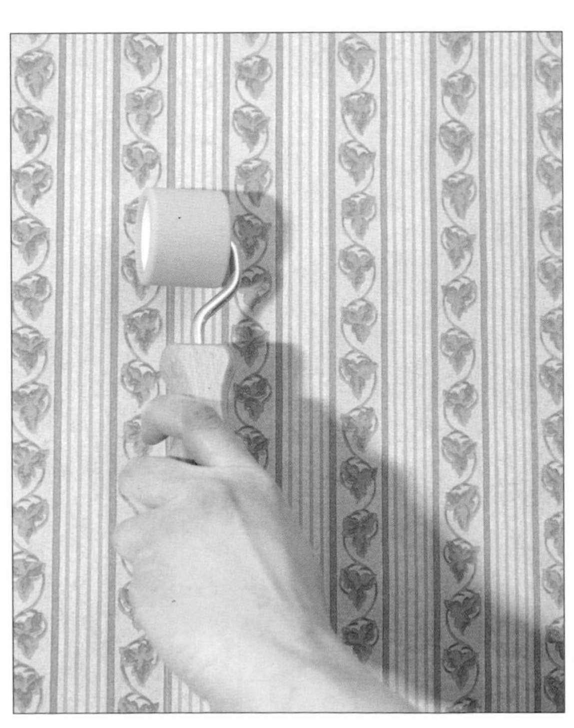

Versatile Living

Many homes today combine the living and dining space, producing a vibrant and versatile room suitable for family life as well as elegant entertaining. Whether your home is large or small, the one-room living space is an attractive and practical way of having a formal seating area in the same place as the relaxed lounge suite.

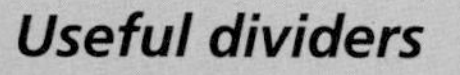

Useful dividers

If you need to divide up a room consider the following options:

- ❖ A floor-length curtain will keep out the draughts
- ❖ Decorate a folding screen to fit in with your decorative scheme
- ❖ Bead or ribbon curtains provide a clever visual partition
- ❖ Place tall bookcases across the space to add double-side storage access

Space need not be a problem if your room is small – there are many styles of table available that can be adapted as needed. The most versatile of these is the round, half-flap table that can be pushed against the wall when not in use, still providing a crescent-shaped surface for letter-writing or dinners for two. Many rectangular tables have additional inserts that allow the tabletop to be extended as required. A flexible size tabletop is useful not only for entertaining varying

▷ This vibrant single-room home can be split into different areas as the need arises. The turquoise folding room divider partitions the living space from the study area while the sleeping section is separated by being raised and concealed on a platform.

numbers of guests or family members, but means that the room can be used as a children's play or work room while other activities take place on the other side of the room.

Lighting considerations for this type of room are very important, and, like the room itself, need to be flexible and suited to every occasion. A light source concentrated over the tabletop is essential if the table is to be used for working or handicrafts, while a more subdued lighting arrangement is better for evening meals. A central light with a dimmer switch would suit both situations. The rest of the room can then be lit as you like, combining lamps, floor lights and wall uplighters for a relaxed ambience.

△ Even if space is at a premium the table can double up as breakfast table in the morning and then become your office desk in the day.

◁ The use of co-ordinating fabrics against a well-matched red background bring the different elements of this room together harmoniously, without any attempt to separate them – the sitting area and dining area fuse together effortlessly. The round table will seat a varying number of people with ease or become a temporary workplace, as the need arises.

Cook's Delight

▽ This sleek white kitchen has plenty of storage space for the cook's utensils and ingredients, with dishes displayed behind an array of frosted glass cabinets.

Every keen cook loves to have everything at his or her fingertips, and the high-tech, gadget-filled kitchen will provide great culinary satisfaction. Even if space is limited, a well-planned kitchen can hold a large number of accessories and appliances and still provide ample storage space and working areas.

Once you have planned what you need in your kitchen, and what is possible in the space that you have, decide on the units or cupboards, the worktops and the type of stove. Consider

your storage requirements – do not forget that you can gain extra space by using a hanging rack or by placing tools and equipment on hooks on a metal wall-mounted grid. Many cupboards now have pull-out sections with deep bins for storing large pots and pans, while every corner can be used to take a rotating storage carousel or small, triangular corner shelving unit.

Do not forget the lighting – you will need to see what you are preparing. Under-cupboard, concealed strip lighting can be very useful for directing light onto the work surface without glaring too brightly into your eyes.

Planning

Careful planning is the key to success. Use a grid to position miniature kitchen pieces until you have the arrangement you like – some kitchen shops will help you do this on computer where you can design everything in 3-D. Be sure that you leave enough space for the various uses the room will have, for example the dining room, children's play area, utility space and general family room. However, remember to indulge the cook's requirements too.

▽ Ingenious storage solutions such as metal racks (top), easy-access open shelving on a corner (centre) and a metal rail attached to the wall for hanging tea towels and pan holders (bottom) all make a kitchen more convenient to use.

◁ A homely, comfortable kitchen, but no less a serious cook's workplace. The flowers and ornaments provide a friendly environment while the open shelving areas allow instant access.

Country Look

∇ Country-style inspiration can be drawn from abroad: this kitchen design has a distinctly Mediterranean look in its colourwashed green cupboards and units and the mixed stone tile floor.

If you live in the country or want to recreate a rustic style, the country kitchen is the perfect room to start. There are many built-in arrangements and designs that use traditional materials in an informal, farmhouse style; you can choose from a vast range of different wooden finishes, from light or dark woods, from flat-fronted cupboards to intricately carved panels with open or closed shelving – the choice is yours.

The floors and walls can be decorated to give a country air. Stone or ceramic flooring slabs or tiles are ideal to complete the visual effect but may not be suitable for every home. Instead choose

from the excellent range of facsimile flooring tiles that resemble granite, terracotta, slate or marble. These provide a much warmer, easy-care surface that is also softer if there are children running about or if you are worried about dropping a favourite piece of crockery or glassware. Wood floors or wooden strip flooring is another attractive alternative.

Walls can be decorated with wallpaper or painted to imitate a rough plaster effect. Check that the wallpaper is resistant to the steam and condensation that can build up in a kitchen.

△ This farmhouse-style kitchen is decorated in a warm apricot shade with a contrasting pea green wash across the beamed ceiling.

△ Wooden chairs, cupboards, dresser bases and serving hatch are combined very effectively with rustic tiles, an old-fashioned range and a porcelain butler's sink to form a perfect country kitchen.

Country touches

- ❖ Hang handstitched samplers on the walls for a homely touch
- ❖ Store and display bright, rustic-style crockery on open shelves
- ❖ Keep bunches of dried herbs on hooks, and grow pots of fresh herbs on the windowsill

Colourwashing

Colourwashing is an extremely versatile technique and looks good almost anywhere. It consists of the application of several layers of colour, one on top of the other. The paint used is diluted so that the other layers or colours show through slightly, giving a loose, translucent effect.

Colourwashing uses broken colour to create different effects, depending on how the paint is brushed on and, equally importantly, how it is treated – or not – at the finishing stages.

The first thing to consider is whether you prefer a strong paint effect or something subtle. Colourwashing is suitable for every type of effect but you will need to experiment a little before settling on your final choice. For a bold finish, consider using a strong colour on a pale background or a dark colour on a slightly lighter base coat, keeping within the same colour range. For a subtle effect, choose lighter colours and combine colours that are near to each other in shade eg beige and cream.

▽ A cloud-like effect is created here using layers of blue and cream paint in fairly large, bold brush strokes. The scheme is completed with a stencilled border.

△ Step 1: Apply two coats of basecoat. When dry, use a large brush to apply the second colour in wide strokes.

△ Step 2: Continue to apply the top coat, building up the effect by overbrushing the previous brush strokes.

△ Step 3: Finally, use a lightly dampened paint brush to smooth out any inconsistencies in the pattern.

Brushing over the finished layers of paint with a very dilute coat of a dusty white colour will 'knock back' the paint and make the overall effect more muted. If you want a glossy finish, apply a gloss water-based varnish.

The size of your brush strokes – and of the brush itself – will also make the pattern more or less obvious. Always brush in a random pattern and use strokes that cross over each other. This will make sure that the paint coverage does not slip into an obvious pattern. When colourwashing you will need to work quite quickly because the paint will soon start to dry. Since the paint is dilute it may be quite runny – simply brush over any drips.

◁ A dilute dark blue is washed over an ivory background in expansive strokes. The impression left by the paint brush adds to the rustic effect of the colourwashing, giving the wall a heavily textured appearance.

You will need

- ❖ Matt emulsion paint in base coat colour
- ❖ Paint roller
- ❖ Paint tray
- ❖ Matt emulsion paint in top coat colour, diluted 50:50 with water
- ❖ Large paint brush

Family Fun

∇ Rather than having laminated cupboard fronts, this kitchen uses the clever disguise for sticky handprints of a pretty blue colourwash over the cabinet doors. The uneven grainy effect hides dirt well, as does the sponging on the wall.

The family kitchen will be a busy place with several different activities taking place in it. There will be many cooks using it, at all levels of height and ability, from toddlers' first cookery lessons and teenagers' experiments with late-night snacks to the chief cook of the family preparing large meals.

Safety and best use of space are going to be prime considerations, as well as the choice of hardwearing, longlasting floors and worktop surfaces. Every surface, from cupboard fronts to door knobs, will have to be wipe-clean. The cupboards and storage units should be designed so that they do not open out onto the main thoroughfare, and they should not have gaps on the hinge side to trap children's fingers. Storage space will need to be carefully thought out, with shelves and cupboards at different heights, with children's toys low down and precious or sharp objects stowed safely high up out of the way.

If you do not have room for a large table, a countertop that doubles as a worktop will do very well as an eating area, perhaps with stools that can be tucked underneath or chairs that can be stacked out of the way. Otherwise think about purchasing a table that folds down to half its size, still providing a small work area against a wall.

Safety first

❖ Fit cupboards containing sharp objects or toxic materials with childproof catches

❖ Do not leave electric cabling trailing – make sure all appliances are fitted with the legal maximum length of cable

❖ Choose different coloured plugs for the various appliances and pieces of equipment

❖ If you have young children, consider fitting a pan guard around the top of the stove

❖ Train young children to keep away from the stove and oven

△ The combination of an exciting colour scheme with materials such as wood, wicker and rush produces a bright, contemporary family room. The hardwearing rush matting is an excellent under table choice and will protect the floor.

△ This practical, country-style family kitchen has plenty of open shelving for large numbers of plates and dishes; the tiled table top is easy to wipe clean, as well as being a cheerful decorative feature.

▷ Good use of space is essential in a family kitchen. Here the dining table is expandable to a larger size for entertaining, and the cooking area is extended by the extra counter that acts as divider and additional worktop.

Living Under Glass

▽ This traditional-style conservatory is spacious enough for it to be used as a study or dining room. The plants are displayed on attractive cast-iron racks in the corners of the room and curving out from one wall. The diamond-pattern marble floor is both elegant and practical.

The conservatory is a wonderful place, full of light and warmth, usually packed with plants and flowers. Although a new conservatory may be fairly costly, it adds so much light and space to the house that it may be a wise addition. It provides not only the perfect place to cultivate cuttings, but also a delightful extension of the sitting room, an all-weather play room for the children or young visitors, and even a romantic spot for a candlelit dinner.

Since the walls and ceilings are usually glass the decorative scheme will concentrate on how to make the most of the light and heat, adapting the room and its furniture so that it can be used in the most versatile of ways. If you install central heating in it, the conservatory can be used in the winter as a suntrap, perfect for relaxing in the warmth in easy chairs. Blinds that can be individually adjusted to shield the eyes from the direct glare of the sun will

△ Clever use of plants and dark green woodwork partially conceals the walls of this conservatory, giving the impression of even greater space. The roller blinds can be adjusted against bright sunlight.

allow you to use the room all day long and will prevent it from becoming unbearably hot in summer.

If you use sealed wooden strip flooring or tiles on the floor, you will not have to worry about spilling water when tending your plants, nor indeed worry about children at play painting or gardening. Rush or sisal matting will also keep the conservatory cool and will look very attractive, but may not be as suitable if the area gets very wet.

▷ The coloured stained glass panels in this conservatory are a striking feature of the decorative scheme. A wide roller blind stretches across the centre roof panel shading eyes and furniture during the brightest hours of sunlight, making the room comfortable to be in at all times of the day.

◁ Not all conservatories are glass on all sides. A cheaper option for urban living is an up-market version of the lean-to, where glass panels extend out from a wall to form a year-round sitting room.

△ If you choose furniture carefully, it will be suitable for both outdoor and indoor living. Cane or wicker furniture looks good anywhere.

Indoors Outdoors

If you enjoy life outdoors, you will no doubt want to try to spend as much time on the patio, terrace or verandah, whether you are reading, watching the children play or having an al fresco meal. The choice of outdoors furniture will be determined by the storage space that you have available. If you can stow table and chairs indoors or under cover when it rains then you have a much wider choice of materials, including wicker or fabric-upholstered chairs, hammocks and canvas director-style seating. If you want something suitable for all climates, choose plastic or wooden furniture – the range is vast and you can select from folding or fixed-frame designs of table and chairs, benches and recliners.

Being outside is marvellous but you will need to consider some form of shade provider; large floral or natural canvas umbrellas, giant Italian wood and cotton parasols and exotic four-poster canopies all look good and provide protection from the sun. There is always the natural choice – a thick, tendrilled vine trained on wires across the patio area. The selection you make will depend on personal taste and on the space available.

▽ Cane and metal furniture always looks very smart outdoors, the natural materials blending in well with the surroundings. This round table is just right for lazy summer meals for two.

△ Be prepared: keep a large hamper filled with picnic cutlery and plates – and of course a corkscrew – for when the sun begins to shine. Just add food and drink and head outside.

Outdoors lighting

❖ If you fit electric lights outdoors, make sure that they are fitted by a professional electrician as the power supply must be properly earthed

❖ Natural light sources include candle flares on tall sticks, nightlights or water candles floating on a bowl of water or in a tub or barrel, and candles in glass jars, perhaps strung on wire from the trees

❖ If you use naked flames or candles, always make sure that you have a fire extinguisher and/or bucket of water handy in case of accidents; make sure each flare or candle is sensibly positioned away from fabric, foliage and twigs

△ This outdoor dining area is well lit with lanterns suspended from a line of cord, while a pretty oval lantern on its own stand hangs over the barbecue.

◁ Brightly coloured crockery complements a meal outdoors perfectly. Mix and match coloured place mats, napkins, china and cutlery for a cheerful summery look.

Home Office

∇ Although this appears to be a traditional incidental table, this small desk can in fact become a useful writing table within seconds, just by moving the ornaments. Paper and pens are concealed in the drawers for instant access.

If you work from home, or just like to have a quiet corner to do the accounts or write a letter or two, you will want to have your own private corner with all that you need to hand. You may not have the space to dedicate a whole room to your workplace, but an area of an existing room can easily be adapted to suit your requirements.

You will probably need a desk or table, and a chair or stool to sit on. A low stool or 'kneeler' chair (which takes the pressure off your back) can be pushed out of the way beneath the desktop when you are not using your work area, particularly useful if it forms part of another room or if space is at a premium. A fold-up or roll-top desk can also be useful in disguising the true nature of the workspace, as can shelves within a cupboard – all your work can be shut away out of sight.

If you can leave your work area undisturbed between sessions, then you will be able to have open shelves, perhaps even a filing cabinet and cupboard unit or two. These need not look like commercial office equipment – there are many elegant designs on the market and a good number look just like living room furniture in stylish wood or laminate finishes. Remember to investigate unusual storage solutions if you have a hobby that demands high-capacity storage; stacking, lidded boxes and metal mesh trolleys are very high-tech and lend a distinct 'designer' look to the room or workspace.

△ This desk has been set up in the bright corner of a living room. The trestles and worktop can be tidied away quickly when extra space is needed or when the office element needs to be hidden.

◁ An attractive and portable wicker stationery holder can be stored in any part of the house without looking out of place.

△ Important elements for the home office: space for books and personal mementoes (top), a good reading lamp (centre) and a comfortable but sturdy chair (bottom).

◁ Stacking boxes in different sizes and colours form practical and decorative storage containers, complete with label holders on the front.

Checks & Stripes

The bedroom is the place to let your decorative scheme take hold. There are so many different patterns and decorative designs to choose from that often the easiest is to take a simple geometric pattern, such as stripes. There are so many forms of the classic stripe: wavy-edged, criss-crossed with another colour to form a loose check, formal and traditional, thick and thin alternating with one another, and the stripe with a flower motif or other pattern running alongside, for example.

△ This room uses a total of five different weights of check in co-ordinating colours, with a striped fabric for the curtain.

Checks and stripes are wonderful to use to stunning visual effect,they can be as restrained or as flamboyant as you please, as traditional or as modern as the mood takes you. Do not be afraid of being adventurous – if you stick to a certain colour range and choose the weight of the different stripes, you can combine several different striped patterns within a single room.

If you want to create a cool but sophisticated bedroom, try contrasting striped fabric on the curtains and bedlinen against a plain-coloured wall, perhaps with just a co-ordinating striped rug on honey-coloured wooden boards.

If, on the other hand, you would like to produce a more striking, colourful effect, try mixing various different weights of stripes in a similar colour range. A pale, almost imperceptible stripe on the wallpaper can be very elegant, especially when it is picked out by the more obvious line of the bedlinen or scatter cushions.

△ Furniture in a room that concentrates on bright patterns for its decorative scheme is best selected in neutral, natural materials.

△ This bedroom uses checks and stripes to calming effect. The striped fabric hanging at the head of the bed is in muted, neutral colours while the bed cover is in a cool olive-based check.

△ Bedlinen and curtains in co-ordinating colours add a fresh feel to this room. The smaller check on the reverse of the bed linen shows how well patterns in different sizes but the same colours can mix.

Using patterns

Do not be afraid to experiment. You can rarely go wrong when mixing checks or stripes if you follow a few simple rules:

❖ Try to keep to a colour theme and only use checks or stripes within a similar range of shades

❖ Mix and match the sizes of checks, from large, bold designs to tiny chequerboard patterns, and choose stripes of different weights

❖ Stripes and checks can be combined to stunning effect as long as the colours do not clash

◁ Bold checks are set against a plain wall in this bedroom. The check pattern is continued in miniature across the wallpaper border, while a larger version is found in the throw on the bedstead.

Ragging

The technique of ragging is fun to apply as it covers an area quickly and you can vary the effect depending on the desired result and the materials you use. Ragging is not complicated and any mistakes are easily concealed within the overall pattern.

Ragging involves the application of an oil-based glaze to a surface and then its removal using a scrunched up piece of chamois leather, cotton fabric or even a piece of old plastic bag, all of which produce a different textured effect. Make sure that the material is free of dust or lint as otherwise any debris may create an uneven pattern or become stuck in the layer of paint.

You will probably be working in sections as you decorate. If you want to avoid having a visible divide in the paint, which may have started to dry by the time you reach subsequent sections, ask someone to help you keep the edges wet. Your helper can add more glaze while you continue with the ragging. This will keep the sections from becoming obvious. While ragging, remember to rescrunch the material regularly and to alter the direction in which you work. This will prevent a pattern repeat from forming. Ragging is a free form

You will need

- ❖ Eggshell paint in basecoat colour
- ❖ Paint brush
- ❖ Paint roller
- ❖ Paint tray
- ❖ Transparent oil glaze, coloured with artist's oil paint
- ❖ Chamois leather
- ❖ Lint-free cotton rag
- ❖ Plastic bag (optional)

△ Step 1: For the basecoat, apply two coats of eggshell, allowing the first coat to dry before applying the second. Working in sections, quickly paint on the glaze.

△ Step 2: Hold a shredded chamois leather rag in your hand and gently remove some of the glaze from the top coat using a light sponging action.

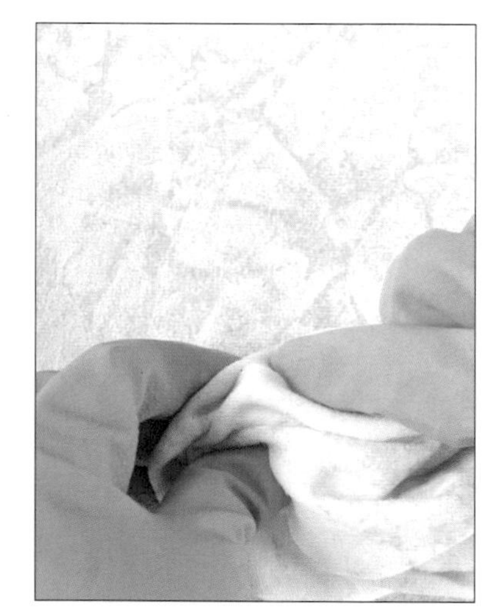

△ Step 3: To soften the ragging patterns and produce a more muted effect, gently press a cotton rag onto the glaze and lift it off, taking off some of the colour.

technique and should be different in every section.

If you want to experiment with colour combinations, ragging is the ideal technique as it uses various layers to build up the final effect. Since the principle of ragging is that of removing wet paint that has been recently applied, any colour that lies behind the top coat will show through in the end result. You can therefore paint the background surface with a colour that is similar to the ragging layer for a subtle effect, or use a strongly contrasting colour, or one that is much lighter or darker, to achieve a variety of bold results.

Try experimenting on pieces of card until you reach a decision about the colours. It is surprising how easily a colour combination can alter an overall effect, making it seem warm or cool, relaxing or invigorating.

△ Ragging has been used to decorate this wall of tongue and groove strips. The mottling produced by the ragging breaks up the strong vertical lines of the wood. The same paint is used as a solid colour to pick out the shelf and washstand.

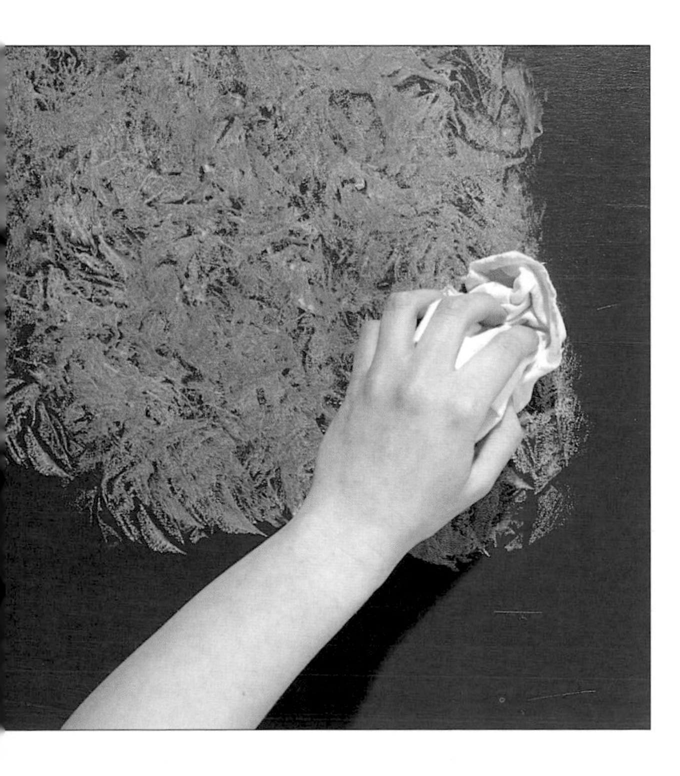

△ Steps 1–3 (left) show the usual ragging technique: that of ragging on. Here, a variation, ragging off, is used to apply a light colour on top of a dark shade.

△ The paint combination, light on dark, looks much bolder when applied with a plastic bag. The crisper edges of the bag produce a much more clearly defined ragging pattern. The edges can be softened or left as they are for a vibrant result.

FLORAL FANCY

△ Use floral designs in the accessories you include in a room to give it a fresh, summery look.

▷ This traditional rose and leaf pattern in the curtain and bedlinen fabric is beautifully co-ordinated with the pale peach-coloured walls, which allow the floral design to make a strong visual impact without becoming overpowering.

One of the most traditional of fabric designs is that of the floral motif. Its variety is endless, whether you prefer a classic rose design, a delicately scattered pattern or a modern abstract. As with stripes, flowers can be combined very effectively, using as daring or as restrained a mixture as you like. The added attraction of floral fabrics is that they always look fresh, particularly if

you like to place a vase of matching flowers in the room to emphasize the decorative motif.

Floral fabrics and wallpapers are available in many co-ordinating ranges, some taking a small theme from one part of the design and repeating it as a delicate pattern on an alternative fabric or paper. Other ranges may incorporate the floral theme with an intricate or brightly coloured background, providing a related but refreshingly different touch.

You will not be restricted to a limited range of colour themes when choosing a floral design; most patterns are produced in many colourways and to suit nearly every taste, even those that veer towards the more masculine range of patterns.

If you want to make a feature of floral fabric or wallpaper, place it in a contrasting position against a pale wall or carpet. Pick out certain colours or themes for the carpets and rugs, and even for stencilled wall decoration. Remember that a patterned fabric will take on a pleasantly different appearance when gathered into curtains, drapes, pelmets and Roman blinds – you may want to continue the use of the fabric into your choice of window dressing for optimum effect.

△ A modern interpretation of the classic floral theme is used in the bedlinen and on the walls.

△ A floral motif can be used in many different sizes. Here a large daisy design is used on one side of the bedlinen and on the pillows, while it appears in varying forms in a patchwork effect on the reverse. A smaller design is found on the walls. The same fabric is used to make matching accessories (right).

Floral accessories

To add just a simple floral touch, or to continue the floral theme, choose from a variety of accessories:

- ❖ Prints and original paintings featuring flower still-life imagery
- ❖ Cushions, pillows and throws in a mixture of floral patterns
- ❖ Pottery with delicate and traditional or bold, modern floral designs

Wood Graining

You will need
- ❖ Eggshell paint in background colour
- ❖ Paint roller/large paint brush
- ❖ Paint tray
- ❖ Transparent oil glaze, coloured with artist's oil paint
- ❖ Rubber rocker
- ❖ Lint-free cotton rag
- ❖ Oil-based varnish

The art of wood graining is an ancient one and was once popular all over Europe in wealthy homes, recreating expensive woods from paint and glazes. Although professional paint-effect artists tend to use a variety of brushes and a whole range of paints and tints, you can imitate wood grain very easily by using a rubber rocker and some coloured oil glaze over eggshell paint as a background.

Wood graining using a rocker is best applied to fairly small areas as the pattern produced is bold and striking, resembling the grain and knots usually found in lengths of pine. The most suitable areas for applying this type of wood graining are along skirting boards, on panels – perhaps going up a staircase or on doors or cupboards – and on small pieces of wooden furniture such as chests or tables which need a little renovation.

Traditional wood graining was normally done in natural wood-like colours, but striking effects can be achieved using bold, primary colours on white or even on a coloured background shade. Experiment on pieces of card with different colour combinations until you find one that suits your purposes best. At the same time take the opportunity to try out the effects of the rocker.

▷ Step 1: Cover the surface with eggshell paint and leave to dry. Apply a top coat of coloured oil glaze. Starting at the top, pull the rubber rocker through the paint, angling it as you pull to achieve variation in pattern (left).

▷ Step 2: Continue to work in smooth strokes, cleaning the rocker ribs after each stroke. Try to vary the position of the widest grain marks for an assymetrical effect. Leave until completely dry then apply a coat of varnish (far left).

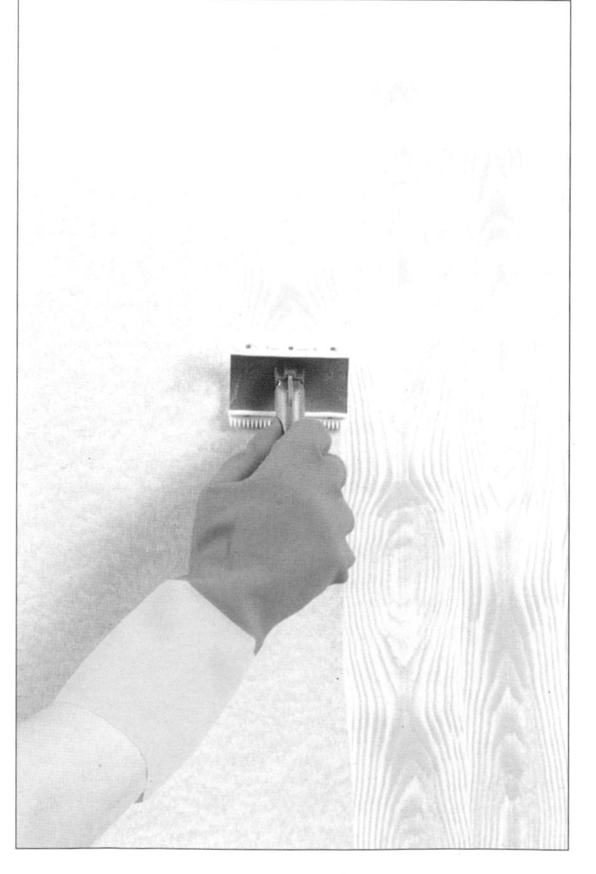

Wood-graining Equipment

Depending on the style of grain you wish to produce, there are various types of equipment available:

- ❖ For a subtle, fine grain, use a mixture of small artist's brushes and paint in the grain by hand on the top coat
- ❖ Experiment with metal or rubber graining combs
- ❖ Use a rocker with a narrow rib or closely arranged set of grooves; these are available in different sizes, with or without a handle

△ Wood graining in a pretty blue shade picks out the panels of the built-in storage space in this bedroom. The background shade is the same as the colour used on the rest of the cupboard doors and on the woodwork in the room, and so helps to create a sense of co-ordinated design.

▽ An opulent effect is easy to create using luxurious piles of cushions in co-ordinating fabrics.

STYLISH SLUMBER

For the most sophisticated of bedrooms, a fair amount of research into decorative styles and types of fabric or wall coverings is required. If you want to recreate a certain period look, such as medieval, Renaissance or Elizabethan, choose fabrics with heraldic and tapestry designs. The same fabric can be used on the bed coverings, on any curtains decorating the bed and for the window dressings. Pile the bed high with cushions and bolsters, each fitted with an ornate cover and perhaps trimmed with silk braid and fringing.

Think about using fabric to create an opulent effect by using it more thickly draped than usual, and extend its use to the upholstery in the room.

If you prefer a more modern bedroom setting, the most sophisticated look is often the most uncluttered, making a feature of an expensive coverlet or quilt or bringing a piece of contemporary furniture – such as an unusual bedstead – to the fore by contrasting it with plain background decoration.

△ A stylish bedroom need not be over-whelming. This pretty red and cream room has an air of elegance and old-fashioned charm, endowed by the simple, double-sided canopy over the bed and the scalloped mattress valance.

Whichever style you opt for, remember to co-ordinate your wardrobes cupboards, and chests of drawers, matching them to the overall design. A 1970s laminated chest of drawers, for example, would look out of place amongst the heraldry and heavy, carved wood of a medieval bedroom suite.

△ This eastern-style room is richly decorated using thick fabrics on the bed, linen chest and – most striking – in the extravagantly draped bed canopy.

▷ A wonderfully stylish medieval-look room has been created here using a subtly stencilled wall and a matching half-tester suspended over the bed.

Bed treatments

- ❖ A four-poster with drapes at each corner is the most elegant and traditional of beds
- ❖ The half-tester style of canopy, whether on posts or hung from the ceiling, is a more unusual method for adding sophistication
- ❖ A corona with full canopy adds a touch of the exotic – add tiebacks and ornate clasps for even greater luxury
- ❖ Lengths of voile gathered above a bed give an air of romantic exoticism to a bedroom setting

Bright And Cheerful

A child's bedroom will serve a dual purpose, especially if two children are sharing it. It must a provide safe and reassuring environment that welcomes the child to sleep at bedtime while also being a play room during the day, with plenty of storage space for toys and games.

Bright colours and simple, bold shapes tend to be the most popular choices for a young child's room, but do not be afraid to be more adventurous in your choice of decorative fabric or wall coverings. There are some very attractive traditional nursery designs available – if they appeal, take home samples and swatches and see how they look in the room.

Wipe-clean surfaces and hardwearing paint finishes are important in a young

△ A bright, modern room, with matching bedlinen, curtains and wallpaper border, perfect for any age child.

▷ A colourful yachting motif is used in different sizes in this welcoming room, both on the walls and in thc fabrics, even in the matching lampshade.

This traditional-style child's nursery uses a classic, teddy-bear theme fabric and wood and wicker furniture (above), all well matched to the colourwashed floor-boards and yellow walls.

child's bedroom. Cupboards and chests of drawers or toy boxes should, ideally, have rounded corners and sturdy, easily grasped handles. Children learn to appreciate books very quickly so include some bookshelves where they can keep their own library.

Decorating the walls of a child's room is always fun; you can let your imagination run wild as you design a bright, adventurous mural or stencil a repeat pattern around the walls. Attaching a frieze at ceiling or dado-rail height is another way of brightening up the room perhaps co-ordinating the design with colours and motifs in the rest of the room.

▷ A baby's room needs to be calming as well as visually stimulating. This design combines different patterns and colours in a charming decorative scheme that will remain suitable as the child grows older.

STENCILLING

Stencilling is a quick and rewarding way of producing an individual paint effect in your home. There is a large selection of pre-cut commercial stencils available in craft shops or from decorators' suppliers, or you can design and cut your own patterns from stiff card or acetate.

The pleasure of stencilling is derived in part from the way in which you can cover large areas of a surface relatively quickly. The complexity of the stencilled pattern and the number of colours used can be varied according to the effect required and the time you have available for decorating. Stencilling is normally done with paints, but you can experiment with special stencilling crayons too. Always make sure that the surface to be decorated is dry and clean, free of dust and grease. Do not rush the work, and remember not to load the brush too heavily with paint.

△ Step 1: If you are cutting your own stencil, draw the design onto a piece of card and secure it to a hard surface using masking tape. Cut out the pattern using a sharp-bladed craft knife, working carefully around any delicate shapes so as not to cut through the card dividing one section from another.

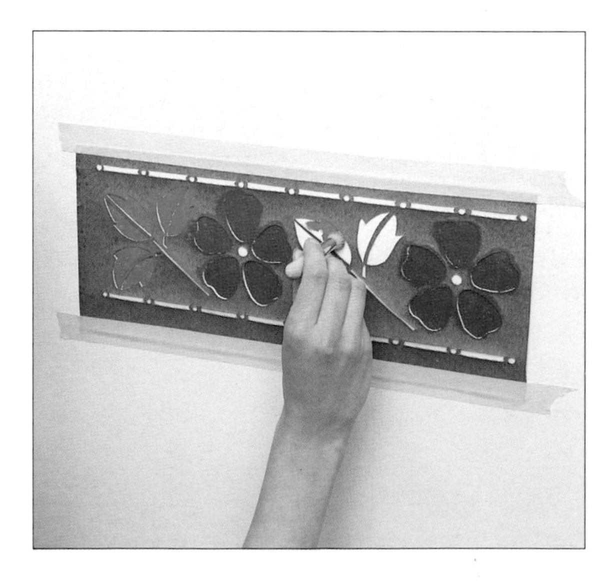

△ Step 2: Using masking tape, secure the stencil to the wall in the required position and begin to paint, using a rapid dabbing motion over the cut area.

△ Step 3: When one section is complete, carefully reposition the stencil, matching the pattern exactly. Continue to paint until the design is finished.

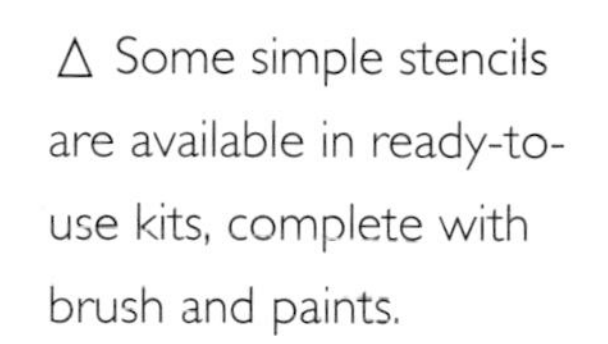

△ Some simple stencils are available in ready-to-use kits, complete with brush and paints.

◁ This simple marine stencil, applied in a single colour, is strikingly effective applied against a colourwashed wooden cabinet, which hangs on a mottled sponged wall.

You will need

- ❖ Pencil
- ❖ Card
- ❖ Masking tape
- ❖ Sharp-bladed craft knife
- ❖ Stencil brush
- ❖ Matt emulsion paints in the required colours

▷ Stencils are perfect for decorating a child's room. These bold yet simple motifs and numbers stand out well against the background of the whitewashed wall, while co-ordinating with the green of the curtain fabric.

Private Den

▽ Perfect for a fashion-conscious teenage girl: the bright colours of the matching flower-motif bedlinen, wallpaper border and curtain fabric are suitable for a variety of ages. The deep orange walls co-ordinate with the orange of the tartan throw kept at the end of the iron bed, which is in an enduring, classical style.

Creating a room for a teenager is more complicated than designing a simple sleeping space. Depending on the age and tastes of your son or daughter, the room will need to be flexible, able to be adapted over the years as the use of the space changes. In the early teen years, games and hobbies will probably take first priority over space for storing and trying on clothes, and there will usually be a constant stream of friends staying over or visiting for the afternoon. Later on, school work, fashion and music may take precedence over games, and the look of the room will take on added importance as awareness of style grows.

The teenager will quickly lend the room a certain individual style and, right from the start, he or she will want to have some input into the styling of the room. Remember to build in extra space for expansion of storage over the years, and choose furniture that will not be considered too childish later on. Try to make the desk area as large as possible,

△ This decorative scheme is an example of a more traditional yet stylish room that will remain well liked even as the teenager grows older.

perhaps building it in under a raised platform bed for extra space and a cabin feel. Wall space will be useful for pictures, posters and pin-ups. If you want to avoid damaging the wall surface why not install pinboards or cover the walls in cork so that every area can be decorated without leaving holes or residue from adhesive putty or tape.

▷ Plenty of floor space, an extra bed for a friend to stay, and even a hammock hanging from a beam: this is a busy teenager's ideal room. Storage space is ample, added even above and below the beds.

▽ This bedroom allows maximum flexibility, with a desk on castors for repositioning as necessary, and a vast amount of storage space. The hanging clothes racks can be concealed by the simple roller blinds.

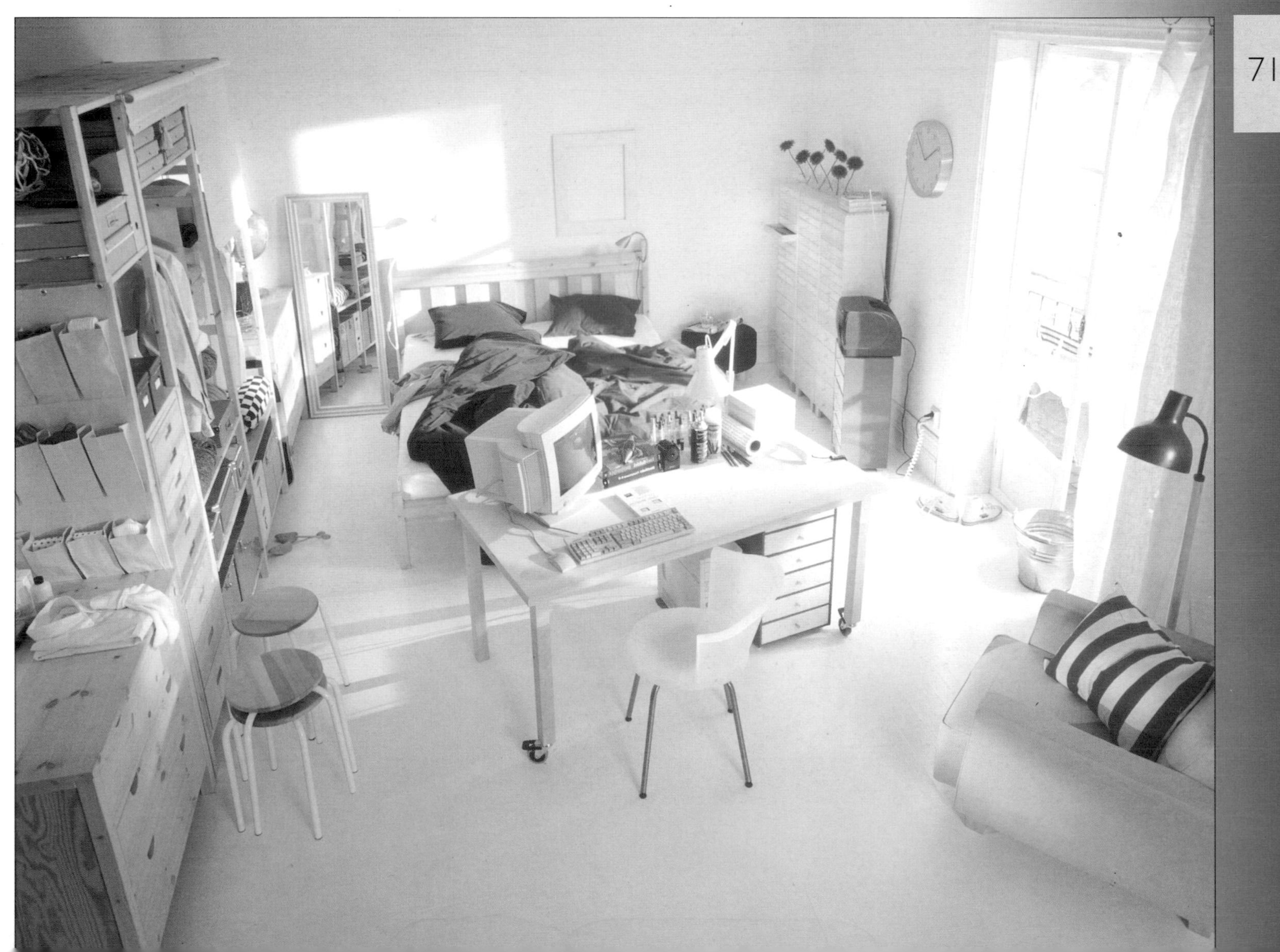

Classic Bathing

Choosing a period-style bathroom is very easy now as there is such a wide range of classic fixtures and fittings. Select either new reproduction pieces or investigate what is available as an original, available from specialist suppliers or architectural salvage companies. If you want to be sure that you remain faithful to a certain period, a little research will soon show which taps or decorative features can be matched with particular sinks or baths.

The bath tub is probably going to provide the main focus of your period bathroom, and you may prefer to go for a classical claw-footed, roll-top bath in cast iron, or to choose an Edwardian style in enamel with an elegant mahogany panelled surround. Choose the taps and shower fitting from a wide range of new or renovated styles, often in chrome or brass, with or without ceramic detail. The shower fitting can be ceramic and hand-held, or choose one of the marvellous large-headed shower attachments that can be fixed within a cubicle.

∇ This elegant bathroom is modelled on traditional lines, with creative use of wooden fittings: the stylish panelling on the walls continues along the side of the bath, and the use of wood is extended to the numerous picture frames, the toilet seat and the collection of boxes.

▷ A feature is made of the bath tub in this decorative scheme. The border picks up the colour of the walls, decorated in a 'print-room' style. The rug and pedestal table give an unusually relaxed and informal feel to the room, despite its traditional appearance.

◁ Wooden panelling need not remain its natural colour when used in a bathroom. The deep green stain used here co-ordinates with the diamond inset tiles on the floor and makes the room lighter than it would be with dark panelling. The scalloped decoration on the suite of bathroom fittings is a pretty touch.

TILING

∇ The tiled chequer-board effect is timeless and blends well even in very modern kitchens. Here it is used on both the wall and floor.

Tiles are hardwearing, waterproof, usually heatproof, and durable. They are available in almost every imaginable style and colour, from reproductions of medieval Italian motifs to modern fluorescent shapes in glass. Plain, textured, matt, glazed or in brilliant relief, the uses of tiles are numerous. Whether you want to use them on wall, floor, inserted in a tabletop or work surface or as a small splashback, you will find the size and shape that is just right.

Most tile manufacturers will let you borrow or buy a sample tile so that you can place it in your home while you consider if you have selected the right design and colour. Tile suppliers and shops will be happy to assist you in calculating how many tiles are needed for a particular area, and should make sure that you receive your tiles from a single batch, unless colour variation is something that you are deliberately aiming for – a patchwork of shades and even different, contrasting colours can be very successful.

Certain tiles are only suitable for particular applications so check with the supplier that your choice is right for where you want to use it.

You will need

- ❖ Tiles to cover area to be tiled
- ❖ Tape measure ❖ Long wooden stick
- ❖ Spirit level ❖ Wooden batten
- ❖ Nails ❖ Small hammer
- ❖ Tile adhesive
- ❖ Tile adhesive spreader
- ❖ Tungsten carbide tile cutter
- ❖ Steel straight edge
- ❖ Tile grout ❖ Grout spreader
- ❖ Small, sharpened stick

◁ This striking kitchen floor is made up of large octagonal tiles cut from a variety of types of stone. The darker diamond-shaped inset tiles balance and link the variation in colours.

△ Step 1: Find the centre point of the area. Calibrate a stick to the size of the tile and use to calculate how many whole tiles will fit.

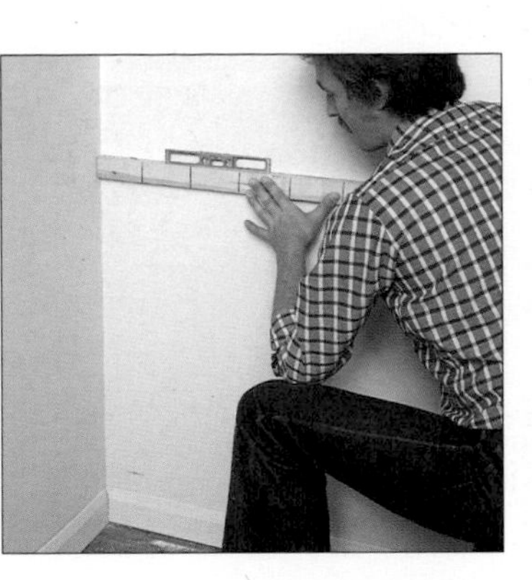

△ Step 2: Mark a horizontal line at the top and bottom of the area. Use the stick and a spirit level to ensure the lines are straight.

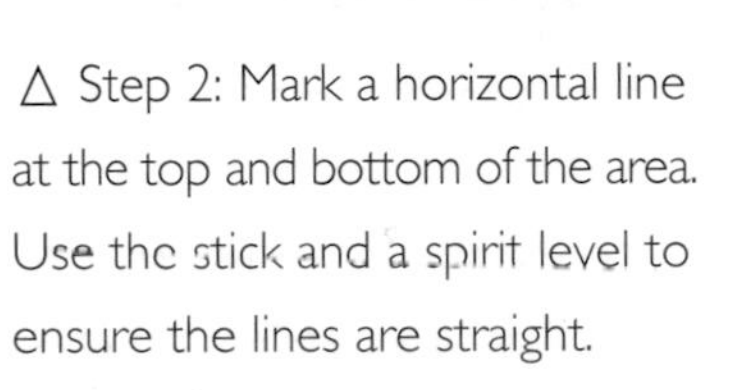

△ Step 3: Nail a wooden batten to the base of the area, beneath the position of the last whole tile. This marks the area of cut tiles.

△ Step 4: Spread tile adhesive on the wall starting in the bottom right-hand corner. Press in the first tile. Work in small sections.

△ Step 5: Continue tiling in small sections, working across the area, until the whole tiles are in place. Remove the batten.

△ Step 6: Allow the adhesive to dry. Place the base of a tile on the bottom of the remaining area and mark the overlap point.

△ Step 7: Strike a line on the tile surface and score through the tile once only using a tile cutter and steel straight edge.

△ Step 8: Snap the tile along the score line, taking care as the edges of the glaze may be sharp. Spread adhesive on the back of the tile.

△ Step 9: Press the tile piece onto the wall, using a slight side-to-side motion to ensure good adhesion. Complete the tiling.

△ Step 10: Allow the adhesive time to dry. Spread tile grout over the tiled area. Any excess can be washed off with warm water.

△ Step 11: Where the grout is uneven or irregular, reshape by running the sharpened stick along the grout lines. Allow to dry.

Warm And Snug

▽ The colours used in this bathroom contribute to its welcoming feel. Deep red walls and cheerful blue and turquoise tiles lift the spirits and give the impression of warmth.

The most welcoming of bathrooms are those that make you want to linger, bathed in warm, tranquil colours and surrounded by family mementoes and little ornaments. Where thick, fluffy towels are always to hand, usually on a traditional wooden drying rack or heated towel rail. The choice of accessories is carefully co-ordinated to extend the decorative scheme. Plants in colourful planters liven up the space, adding a splash of sharp green to the colours of the walls and bathroom suite.

Achieving this cosy look does not necessarily mean incurring great expense. Imaginative use of paint and

tiles on the walls will immediately enliven a dull, old bathroom, even if you cannot manage to purchase a new bathroom suite. Add individual touches such as a paint effect, perhaps stencilling on 'tiles' or sponging a subtle and delicate colour shade on top of a base coat, or add some tongue and groove strips up to dado-rail height, finishing them off with a translucent colourwash.

Whenever possible remember to use special water-resistant bathroom paint when decorating the walls, or protect paint effects with a couple of coats of varnish – the effects of condensation and steam will act more quickly in a bathroom than elsewhere.

△ This decorative scheme is based on the inventive use of tiles: they are placed at an angle on the walls but are fitted in straight lines on the floor.

Light touches

❖ Decant bath oils into pretty glass or ceramic containers for a modern look

❖ Fresh flowers in an unusual vase add a lively touch

❖ Co-ordinate your towels, washcloths and accessories for real designer decor

❖ Choose fun soap dishes and toothbrush holders in bright or co-ordinating colours

▷ Deep shades of blue and golden yellow form the basis of this bathroom scheme, where contrasting patterns are placed in daring combination.

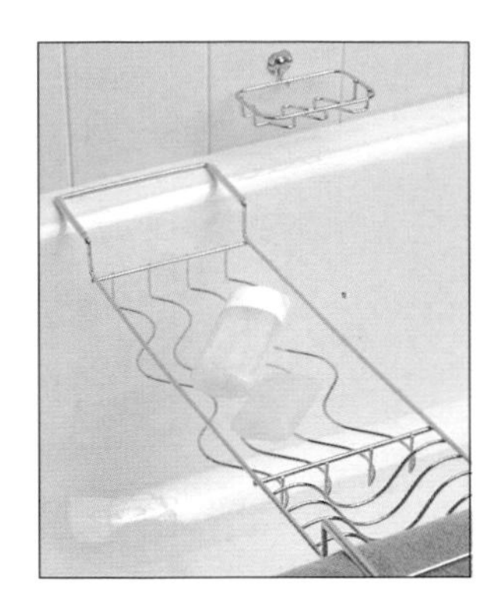

△ Stainless steel accessories such as this bath rack and soap dish add minimalist chic to your bathroom style.

Cool Moods

If you long for cool, uncluttered space with sleek lines and a look that will never date, design your bathroom along beautiful, minimalist lines. You can shut yourself away from the rest of the house and your daily routine, and relax amongst the smooth curves and modulated light of your own private, designer-look space.

It is easy to produce an impressive, expensive-looking bathroom at relatively low cost, but you do need to be disciplined about what goes into it. Choose your accessories carefully and do not allow yourself to get carried away. Conceal anything extra in built-in cupboards or concealed, panelled storage units fitted flush with the walls, perhaps with spring catches rather than prominent handles which can distract the eye from the overall look.

The bathroom suite should be designed along smooth curves, without elaborate moulding. Taps and other fittings should co-ordinate – choosing an unusual designer-style of tap will immediately add to the bathroom fixtures. Matching towel holders, soap dishes, bath accessories and toothbrush containers will extend the range.

Keep the walls fairly plain, perhaps adding only a touch of contrast with a single line of coloured tiles or occasional stencilled motif. The most striking paint effects in a room of this sort are carefully muted stonework or rough plaster designs often in neutrals or dark granite tones.

◁ Deep primary colours on the walls and floors form the perfect setting for this unusual sunken bath.

Designer element

If you want to add one startling element to the bathroom, choose from the new ranges of sculptural towel rails, their heated racks criss-crossing in elaborate panels up and down the wall. The towel rails are available in a range of sizes and finishes, from bright primary colours to metallics and mattes. Practical as well as decorative, they immediately add an air of contemporary chic.

▷ Here neutral colours on the floor and walls provide a backdrop for the double-width shower, complete with fold-down wooden seat.

▽ Clean lines and cool colours form the basis of this scheme, with elements borrowed from the Shakers, famous for their simplicity of design.

△ To achieve a totally co-ordinated look, use accessories and containers in unusual designs, such as these elegant spongeware ceramic pots in green and white.

Flying High

If you want to extend your living area, try looking upwards. You may have a marvellous roof or loft area that requires only the addition of windows or skylights to make it into a wonderful new living room, bedroom or study.

Many homes have walk-in lofts or attics that may have never reached their full potential. Other houses may be perfect for conversion – but do remember to check out the local planning requirements first. Depending on your needs and design preferences, you can either incorporate existing features of the space – such as exposed beams, wooden flooring and the sloping eaves – or model a modern living space that is light and airy.

△ This attic space has been converted into a child's bedroom and play area. Rather than trying to conceal the sloping roof and eaves, a decorative feature has been made of them using a juxtaposition of different wallpaper designs and a bright border which matches the curtain fabric.

Some roof spaces will inevitably have some areas where the ceiling slopes, and judicious decorating can certainly lend an atmosphere of warmth and closeness to what might otherwise be a dark, cramped space. If you paint the room in pale, light tones it will immediately look larger and feel airier. On the other hand, for a den-like feel, painting the whole room, both walls and ceiling, in reassuring earthy hues will provide unity and add depth to the area. Spend some time considering how best to light the space – carefully placed spotlights can pick out certain areas of the room while leaving others more muted.

Do not be put off by the thoughts of wasted space in nooks and crannies – roof rooms are perfect for experimenting with storage ideas. Even the smallest under-eave space can take fitted shelves or specially made, built-in cabinets, while partitioning off corners and angles with sets of cupboard doors provides an instant concealed storage area.

△ Here too the wallpaper border marks the slope of the ceiling yet the smaller room space is made to seem larger by use of an overall background colour.

Roof space uses

Use the additional space for a variety of uses:

❖ Extra living room space for television watching or games
❖ A guest bedroom, perhaps with sink or private bathroom
❖ Study space, with room for a computer and fax machine
❖ Extended storage space for stowing away less frequently used or bulky belongings

△ The original structural features of this roof-space have been incorporated into the design of this bathroom. The exposed beams, casement window and polished wooden floorboards help to retain the cottage atmosphere of the house.

◁ Colourwashing the wooden beams and planks of the steeply sloping ceiling in the same colour as the walls has added a sense of space to this lofty bedroom. The round windows let in a lot of light so the room never seems cramped.

Storage Solutions

△ A sturdy wicker basket can be used to store and transport crockery, both indoors and out, especially if you like dining outside in the summer.

▽ This inexpensive but stylish fabric shelf stack is ideal for storing children's clothes and toys. It can be folded up and tidied away so makes a perfect temporary wardrobe.

Your home is probably already filled with storage spaces, even if you do not realize it. Look around – all the items of furniture that you take for granted such as shelves, desks and ordinary cupboards can all be made to work that little bit harder. Every shelf can have smaller storage boxes, CD or cassette racks, collectors' trays and pots for trinkets, pens and pencils stowed away on it. Every cupboard can contain wonderfully bright and sturdy lidded stacking boxes to hold anything from towels and bedlinen to children's toys and hobby supplies. Wooden trunks and pretty wicker baskets can provide essential storage while also adding coherence to a decorative scheme.

Every alcove can hold shelving and odd angles and corners under the stairs – or in the stairwell itself – can take a traditional wooden corner cupboard or open cabinet. Make the most of space under beds – make or buy rolling wooden drawers for storing shoes, magazines or clothes, or toys in the children's rooms. Decorate the drawers to match the decor of the room so that they form part of the scheme, fitting in effortlessly with the rest of the furniture, or conceal them behind a pretty valance.

▷ Make the most of storage space in the kitchen by incorporating many small drawers of different sizes instead of the usual single-drawer cabinets.

Storage today is a booming design area. Your choice is vast: from hanging fabric shelves to shiny metal document boxes, from traditional wicker baskets to printed cardboard self-assembly magazine holders – there is something to suit every taste and every room. Whether you need home office or bathroom storage containers, or kitchen racks and hanging holders, you will delight in doing the research alone.

◁ Extra shelves always provide an excellent display and storage option. Here the shelves have been built in around the doorway, framing the entrance to the room without detracting from the space available within the room. A feature has been made of the shelves by the addition of sponged red paint on the walls, which form an attractive continuous backdrop to the items on display.

△ Storage space in a bedroom can blend into the overall decorative scheme. Here the linen chest and alcove shelving form an integral part of the room.

Handy storage hints

When buying storage containers for a particular room, first investigate items intended for a different room entirely. You will be surprised how easily one container can be used for another use. For example, stacking vegetable racks intended for the kitchen will look great in the bathroom, piled high with luxurious towels, scented soaps and a few magazines for that long soak in the bath. Metal filing boxes meant for office use will be perfect in the kitchen for holding recipe cards, shopping lists and even spices.

△ A three-tier metal rack with basket and butcher's hooks provides versatile kitchen storage.

Lighting Choices

△ Simple but stylish lamps look good in a variety of rooms.

▽ Traditional lighting for a classical sitting room: these elegant table lamps cast enough light for evening reading.

The lighting you choose for each room will create and affect the ambience within. As well as atmosphere, you should consider the practical applications when lighting each area, matching the type of light source to the aesthetic style of the light fitting itself. For example, in a period-style or traditional room you will probably want to select a classic style of lamp or light fitting, while in a modern room you are more likely to choose from one of the many contemporary or designer ranges of lighting.

However, on the other hand, stunning effects can be created by combining starkly modern lights with more traditional furniture, so have fun looking

through catalogues and brochures to explore the ranges available.

The type of light that you choose will depend ultimately on its intended function. The home office will need a clear light source directed on the work area, and in a relaxing living room wall-mounted or floor uplighters can provide a general light source while tall floor lamps or down beams can pinpoint light onto a favourite reading or sewing chair.

Kitchens need gentle light over the main dining area (if it is incorporated into the kitchen space) and more direct beams on the preparation and work surfaces. Under-cupboard lights can work well in this case, the fittings being hidden from view by the cupboard plinths.

Bathroom lighting

The mood of a bathroom can be altered dramatically by the type of lighting, and you will need different light types at different times of the day. For shaving, fitting contact lenses and putting on make up you will need a good light probably positioned over the sink, while for an evening bath wall-washing sconces and even a few candles will be perfect.

▽ This kitchen is lit mainly by the natural light streaming in from the split level balcony windows above, yet for extra illumination and evening light halogen spots are directed onto work and dining areas.

△ Lamps and uplighters come in a variety of styles to suit every scheme.

△ For a sophisticated central ceiling light, a period-style glass shade is an excellent choice.

Fun With Fabrics

△ Enliven a room with the simple addition of cushions made up in patterned fabrics, in colours that co-ordinate with the existing decorative scheme.

Adding a new fabric to a room is a marvellous way of brightening up the decor without necessarily redecorating the whole room or spending a great deal of money. There are so many different fabric ranges available now that all you have to do is a little bit of research, decide upon the look you want and off you go – a new, chic room!

Before you make your final choice of fabric, take home several different samples and swatches, the bigger the better. This way you will be able to place the fabric in your home, in the position where it will be used, and you can live with it for a few days while deciding if it is the one for you. Most shops are happy to provide swatches, although you may

△ This window is immediately given a new lease of life with fresh green curtains with a white leaf motif.

◁ Fabric can add a sumptuous air to a room. This curtain fabric with its golden tassels has a trompe l'oeil effect and blends in with the red decor.

be expected to return very large sample. Taking samples home means that you can be sure of your choice before you buy the final quantity, so avoiding expensive mistakes.

You can use fabric to enliven windows, old sofas and armchairs and to recover cushions. It can even be used to cover walls, although this takes a bit more time since it will need to be applied very carefully. A new pair of curtains or a beautiful blind will lift a room completely, especially with a delicate set of sheer undercurtains set in front of the panes to produce a more subdued and elegant light.

Fabric types

Choose from:

❖ Tapestry and brocades for a traditional look

❖ Toile de Jouy and seventeenth-century monochromatic designs for a light but classic appeal

❖ Bright and modern prints and linen weaves for the contemporary touch

❖ Mixtures of 'naturals', popular for giving a designer, minimalist look to a living area

△ This bed has been made into the centre-piece of the room with the addition of cheerful yellow covers.

◁ Before deciding on a final fabric choice, take home large swatches and try mixing and matching them against the existing colours and patterns.

Flooring Variety

△ Floor tiles are available in a wide variety of sizes, designs and materials to suit all practical uses and styles of decor.

▽ If you have wooden floorboards in your home but do not want to sand and varnish them, apply several coats of emulsion paint and then varnish.

When you are choosing flooring for a particular area of your home, you will need to consider several factors; the wear and tear sustained in the room, the practical considerations such as cleaning and what might come into contact with the floor area as well as cost, safety and style.

There are many different types of flooring available today. Ceramic, slate or terracotta tiles come in a variety of sizes; some need sealing or waxing while others are glazed and just require a quick mopping down. Cork tiles and wood strip flooring produce a warm, natural-looking effect, and can even be cleaned using a vacuum cleaner. Although a kitchen is normally fitted with tiles, linoleum, vinyl floor covering or shallow-pile carpet tiles – which often have built-in stain resistance – are also an excellent choice.

Carpets of all types, colours and costs are available, with or without fitting costs included in the price. Coir, sisal and seagrass matting are also very popular and look right in both a modern and a traditionally styled home.

Matting comes in a wide variety of weaves and textures; before making your final choice, take home some samples and try walking on each type in bare feet – you will be astonished at the different sensations and will no doubt prefer some textures to others.

△ Tiles produce a decorative effect as well as being a practical choice for an area such as a bathroom that receives a lot of wear and tear.

▷ Carpet is a good choice for a child's room, providing a soft play surface and offering a certain amount of soundproofing during riotous games.

Rug risks

Be very careful about where you position rugs around the house. Never place them at the top of staircases or in other places where they could be a tripping hazard.

Generally speaking, rugs should not be placed on shiny floor surfaces; however, there are now several effective types of rug underlay available which can be placed on the floor beneath the rug or attached to the rug itself, on the underside. This underlay reduces the risk of the rug slipping out from under foot as you step onto it.

Λ Neutral textured carpeting is hardwearing and attractive, and it co-ordinates well with any scheme.

Wonderful Walls

▽ Contrasting patterns of wallpaper in co-ordinating colours can be combined effectively within a design scheme. Here a wallpaper with a small motif design is used above the Celtic-style border, with a striped pattern beneath.

Even if you do not want to re-design all the rooms of your home, fresh wall paints or papers can give new life to tired decor. There are many ranges of both paint and paper available so it is worth taking a bit of time for research. Take home paint charts and wallpaper samples and view them with your furniture. Remember to look at the colours both in natural light by a window as well as beneath the light sources in the rooms you want to decorate. A paint colour will usually appear slightly darker when it is on the wall.

When you have narrowed down your choice, go back to the supplier and ask for a sample pot. Paint a patch on the wall you want to paint and live with the colour for a few days, seeing if it is the right choice for that room. You may well choose a couple of shades and paint sample patches of them both. Sample pots can save the time and money that might be spent rectifying mistakes later.

If you prefer wallpaper, hang a sample piece in the room and see if you really like it in place. If you are considering a border, take a sample of this too and also place it in the room. Experiment with a combination of co-ordinating designs – you may decide to be daring and leave some walls plain while using a pattern on the other sides.

▷ A two-colour painted design adds an individual touch to this bathroom. The bath is cleverly incorporated into the scheme by the continuation of the blue paint from the wave pattern on the walls onto the tongue-and-groove panelling.

Paint effects

These give a very individual style to a room and can be a unique way of combining colours in a daring fashion. Choose from :

- ❖ Spattering or mottling
- ❖ Marbling or woodgraining
- ❖ Sponging or ragging
- ❖ Colourwashing and rubbing back
- ❖ Trompe l'oeil and murals
- ❖ Stencilling or stamping

△ These rooms have been decorated using subtle variations of pattern within the same colour ranges, with a leafy border leading the eye up around the door frame.

◁ For a paint-effect style, choose a wallpaper that mimics colour-washing, stencilling or sponging.

Finishing Touches

△ Even the most casual of items brighten a room.

▽ These accessories have been selected to match the rest of the room in colour and style .

Accessories and ornaments give a home its unique, individual style and reflect your personal tastes. Cushions, pictures, vases and pottery make a room welcoming, homely and interesting while revealing a little about you as a person of style.

You may choose accessories for a particular room, or you may prefer to collect objects that you find pleasing and useful and place them in the room that you feel is most suited to their design. Obviously, certain rooms require certain types of accessory, such as the kitchen or bathroom, but even then the surprise choice is often very successful. Painted flowerpots to hold soap and washcloths do not look out of place in the bathroom, while a log basket in the bedroom to hold magazines or sweaters will look wonderfully rustic.

△ A collection of ornaments and furniture in a similar style rounds off a design scheme perfectly.

Sometimes the accessories in your home form part of a prize collection: teapots, Wedgwood china, model cars or even first edition paperback books all form a marvellous visual display while brightening up a room and revealing something about your interests.

Even the most practical of objects can count as an accessory. Cushions, fruit bowls and candlesticks are all useful in their own right, but the choice of colour, texture and design is where you can let your styling instincts have free reign. Think about including unusual items and see just what stylish designs you can find; doorstops, boot scrapers, draught excluders and book ends are all available in the most diverse and unusual versions, some amusing and some beautifully traditional. Choose whichever suits your decorative scheme or just your sense of fun.

◁ A feature has been made here of simple terracotta flowerpots on a plain white shelf. They show up well against the stencilled striped wall behind.

△ Wrought iron pieces add a certain style to a room: here the mirror frame and the corner shelves are of the same design and work well placed together.

◁ The accessories in this bathroom follow a theme, that of natural materials. The plants are in varying sizes of terracotta pot, while the clay pedestal dish is filled with scented dried orange slices.

SUPPLIERS' ADDRESSES UK

Accessories

The Holding Company
243-245 Kings Road
London SW3 5EL
Tel: 0171 352 1600

The General Trading Company
144 Sloane Street
London SW1X 9BL
Tel: 0171 730 0411

Jerry's Home Store
163-167 Fulham Road
London SW3 6SN
Tel: 0171 580 0909

Next Interiors
Gedding Road
Leicester LE5 4DW
Tel: 0116 284 9424

Nice Irma's
46 Goodge Street
London W1P 1FJ
Tel: 0171 580 6921

The Pier
200 Tottenham Court Road
London W1P 9LD
Tel: 0171 836 9843

David & Charles Wainright
61/63 Portobello Road
London W11 3DB
Tel: 0171 727 0707

Bathrooms

Armitage Shanks
Armitage
Rugeley
Staffordshire WS15 4BT
Tel: 01543 490253

CP Hart
Newnham Terrace
Hercules Road
London SE1 7DR
Tel: 0171 902 1000

Dolphin Fitted Bathrooms
Bromwich Road
Worcester WR2 4BD
Tel: 01905 748500

Doulton and Twyfords
Lawton Road
Allsager
Stoke-on-Trent ST7 2DF
Tel: 01270 410023

Ideal Standard
The Bathroom Works
National Avenue
Kingston-upon-Hull
HU5 4HS
Tel: 01482 346461

Mira
Cromwell Road
Cheltenham
Glos. GL52 5EP
Tel: 01242 221221

Bedrooms

Dorma
PO Box 7
Lees Street
Swinton
Manchester
M27 6DB
Tel: 0161 794 4781

The Iron Bed Company
Summer Carr Farm
Thornton-le-Moor
Northallerton
North Yorks DL6 3SG
Tel: 01609 778143

Sharps Bedrooms
Albany Park
Camberley
Surrey GU15 2PL
Tel: 01276 802000

Silks Bedrooms
PO Box 69
Brierley Hill
West Midlands DY5 1YD
Tel: 0500 474557

Conservatories

Anglian Windows
PO Box 65
Norwich
Norfolk NR6 6EJ
Tel: 01603 787000

BAC Conservatories
Edinburghs Drive
Eastern Avenue
West Romford
Essex RM7 7PX
Tel: 01708 729829

Marston & Langinger
192 Ebury Street
London SW1W 8LP
Tel: 0171 824 8818

Oak Leaf Conservatories
Clifton Common
Industrial Park
Kettlestring Lane
York
North Yorks YO3 8XF
Tel: 01904 690401

Curtain Poles and Ironwork

Artisan
4A Union Court
20-22 Union Road
London SW4 6JP
Tel: 0171 498 6974

Fabric

Anna French
343 Kings Road
London SW3 5ES
Tel: 0171 351 1126

Crowson Fabrics
Crowson House
Bellbrook Park
Uckfield
E. Sussex TN22 1QZ
Tel: 01825 761055

Harlequin Fabrics and Wallcoverings
Cossington Road
Sileby
Leics LE12 7RU
Tel: 01509 816575

Homestyle
AG Stanley Ltd
Victoria Mills
Macclesfield Road
Holmes Chapel
Crewe
Cheshire CW4 7PA
Tel: 0990 133610

John Wilman Fabrics and Wallcoverings
Riverside Mills
Crawford Street
Nelson
Lancs BB9 7QT
Tel: 01844 261800

Malabar
The Coach House
Bakery Place
119 Altenburg Gardens
London SW11 1JQ
Tel: 0171 978 5848

Ian Mankin
109 Regent's Park Road
London NW1 8UR
Tel: 722 0997

The Natural Fabric Company
Wessex Place
127 High Street
Hungerford
Berks RG17 0DL
Tel: 01488 684002

Sanderson
112-120 Brompton Road
London SW3 1JJ
Tel: 0171 584 3344

Flooring

Allied Carpets
Crayfield House
Main Road
St Paul's Cray
Orpington
Kent BR5 3HP
Tel: 0181 466 4006

The Carpet Council Advisory Service
1 Chelsea Manor Gardens
London SW3 5PN
Tel: 0171 349 0773

Crucial Trading
4 St Barnabas Street
London SW1W 8PE
Tel: 0171 730 0075

Fired Earth
Twyford Mill
Oxford Road
Adderbury
Oxon OX17 3HP
Tel: 01295 812088

Floor Coverings International
High Quality House
Sandbeck Way
Wetherby
Yorks LS22 7DN
Tel: 01937 588456

Hardwood Flooring Co Ltd
146/152 West End Lane
London NW6 1SD
Tel: 0171 328 8481

Junkers
Wheaton Court
Commercial Centre
Wheaton Road
Witham
Essex CM8 3UJ
Tel: 01376 517512

Wood 'N Floors
186 Chingford Mount Road
Chingford
London E4 9BS
Tel: 0181 559 4599

Furniture

Grange
PO Box 18
Stamford
Lincs DE9 2FY
Tel: 01780 54721

Habitat
196 Tottenham Road
London W1P 9LD
Tel: 0171 225 2545

Heal's
196 Tottenham Road
London W1P 9LD
Tel: 0171 636 6111

Ikea
2 Drury Way
North Circular Road
London NW10 0TH
Tel: 0181 208 5600

Garden Furniture

Delta Garden Furniture
NAG Business Centre
1 Bank Chambers
Central Avenue
Sittingbourne
Kent ME10 4AE
Tel: 01795 530500

Pepe Garden Furniture
Burhill
Buckland
Near Broadway
Worcs WR12 7LY
Tel: 01386 858842

Viceroy (Kent) Ltd
PO Box 13
Wingham
Canterbury
Kent CT3 1PJ
Tel: 01227 720291

Kitchens

Alno (UK) Ltd
Unit 10
Hampton Farm Industrial Estate
Hampton Road West
Hanworth
Middx TW13 6DB
Tel: 0181 898 4781

English Kitchen Company
Dean House
Suthers Street
Off Featherstall Road
Werneth
Oldham OL9 7TH
Tel: 0161 627 0042

Magnet
Royd Ings Avenue
Keighley
West Yorkshire BD21 4BY
Tel: 01535 661133

Moben Fitted Kitchens
2 Brindley Road
Old Trafford
Manchester M16 9HQ
Tel: 0161 872 2422

Underwood Kitchens Ltd
Unit 2
Lawn Farm Business Centre
Grendon Underwood
Bucks HP18 OQX
Tel: 01296 770043

Lighting

Acorn Lighting Products Ltd
22 Kings Road
Shalford
Guildford
Surrey GU4 8JU
Tel: 01483 564180

Loft Conversions

Priory Loft Conversions Ltd
Priory House
24 Brighton Road
Salfords
Red Hill RH1 5BX
Tel: 01293 774580

Velux
Woodside Way
Glenrothes East
Fife KY7 4ND
Tel: 01592 772211

Paint and Paint Effects

Crown Paints
Technical Advice Centre
PO Box 37
Crown House
Hollins Road
Darwen
Lancs BB3 0BG
Tel: 01254 704951

Dulux
ICI Paints Division
Wexham Road
Slough
Berks SL2 5DS
Tel: 01753 550555

The English Stamp Company
Sunnydown
Worth Matravers
Dorset BH19 3TP
Tel: 01929 439117

Farrow & Ball
33 Uddens Trading Estate
Ferndown
Wimbourne
Dorset BH21 7NL
Tel: 01202 876141

Homestyle
AG Stanley Ltd
Victoria Mills
Macclesfield Road
Holmes Chapel
Crewe
Cheshire CW4 7PA
Tel: 0990 133610

Laura Ashley
150 Bath Road
Maidenhead
Berks SL6 4YS
Tel: 01686 622116

Paint Magic
79 Shepperton Road
London N1 3DF
Tel: 0171 354 9696

Stencil Store
20-21 Herongate Road
Chorleywood
Herts WD3 5BN
Tel: 01923 285577

Wallcoverings

Coloroll
Riverside Mills
Crawford Street
Nelson
Lancs BB9 7QT
Tel: 01844 261800

Homestyle
AG Stanley Ltd
Victoria Mills
Macclesfield Road
Holmes Chapel
Crewe
Cheshire CW4 7PA
Tel: 0990 133610

John Wilman Fabrics and Wallcoverings
Riverside Mills
Crawford Street
Nelson
Lancs BB9 7QT
Tel: 01844 261800

Sanderson
112-120 Brompton Road
London SW3 1JJ
Tel: 0171 584 3344

SUPPLIERS' ADDRESSES USA

Fabric

Decor Home Fashion Inc
140 58th Street
Brooklyn
New York 11220

Flooring and Tiles

American Ocean Tile Company
1000 Cannon Avenue
Lansdale
Pennsylvania 19446
Tel: 215 855 1111

Armstrong World Industries
PO Box 3001
Lancaster
Pennsylvania 17603
Tel: 800 233 3823

Crossville Ceramics
Box 1168
Crossville
Tennessee 38557
Tel: 615 484 2110

Furniture

Bernhard Woodworking Ltd Inc.
3670 Woodhead Drive
Northbrook
Illinois 60062

Shelves and Cabinets Unlimited
7880 Dunbrook Road
San Diego
California 92126

Tools, Equipment and Paint

Builders Square Inc.
9725 Datapoint Drive
San Antonio
Texas 70229

Home Depot
2727 Paces Ferry Road
Atlanta
Georgia 30339
Tel: 404 433 8211

JC Penney
1301 Avenue of the Americas
New York
New York 10019
Tel: 212 222 6161

Porter Cabel Corporation
4825 Highway
45 North Jackson
Tennessee 38302

Sears Roebuck
Sears Tower
Chicago
Illinois 60684
Tel: 800 366 3000

Stanley Tools
1000 Stanley Drive
New Britain
Connecticut 06053

Wallpaper

Crown Wallcovering Corp.
20 Horizon Boulevard
South Hackensack
New Jersey 07606

Mazer's Discount Home Centers Inc.
210 41st Street South
Birmingham
Alabama 35222

PICTURE CREDITS

The Publisher would like to thank the following sources for their kind permission to reproduce the photographs in this book:

Addition Public Relations: **Coram** 79 top right, 93 bottom left; **Homestyle** 4, 9 bottom, 11 top right, 6 left of centre, 19 top left, 20-21, 25 bottom, 46, 47 bottom left, 59 top right, 77 bottom left, 80 left and right, 84 top left, 85 bottom right, 90 left and bottom, 91 bottom, 93 top.
Jon Bouchier 18.
Camron Public Relations: **Coloroll** 60 top left; **Doulton** 88 bottom right; **Grange** 1, 81 bottom; **The Holding Company** 54 right, 55 bottom, 82 top left, 83 bottom right; **John Wilman Fabrics and Wallpapers** *'La Scala'* Collection 86 bottom left, 92 bottom right, *'Poetry'* Collection 8 right, 13 left of centre, 22 top left and left of centre, 49 top right, 55 left, top right, right of centre and bottom right, 64 top left and left of centre, 86 top left, 92 top left; **The Pier** 14, 49 left and bottom right, 51 bottom left, 52 top and bottom right, 53 top, 79 bottom right, 82 bottom left; **Twyfords** *'Provencal'* 77 top, *'Rhapsody'* 79 bottom left.
John Cook: 75.
Crowson: *'Jewels of India'* Collection 64 right of centre, *'Mardi Gras'* Collection 19 top right, 34, 87 left, *'Petite Fleur'* Collection 60 right, *'Renaissance'* Collection 30, *'Royal Pavilions'* Collection 22-23.
Simon de Courcy Wheeler: 18, 38.
Andrew Dee: 39 top left and top right, 45 bottom left, 59 bottom left and bottom right, 67 top left and top right, 74 bottom right.
Fired Earth: 16 bottom, 17 bottom right, 75 bottom right, 84 bottom.
GCI Croup: **The Carpet Council** 9 top, 11 top left, 21 top, 89 top right and bottom.
H&R Johnson Tiles Ltd: Geometric Range *'Exeter'* 20 left, *'Monmouth'* 88 top left.
Harlequin Fabrics and Wallcoverings Ltd: 28 top left, left of centre, bottom left and right, *'Amorini'* Collection 8 left, 29 right, 41, 88 bottom left, *'Celtia'* Collection 65, *'Cornucopia'* Collection 31, 36 right, 48 left, 83 bottom left, *'Floraganza'* Collection 10, *'Flower Garden'* Collection 36 left, *'Hullabaloo'* Collection 15 right, 67 bottom, *'Midsummer'* Collection 2-3, 7 top left, *'Plains and Stripes'* Collection 91 top, *'Santa Fe'* Collection 12, 37, *'Tavani'* Collection 83 top.
Carnival Fabrics and Wallcoverings: *'Copacabana'* Collection 7 top right, 70 right, 92 bottom left, *'Piccolo'* Collection 13 right, 35 main, top right, above centre, below centre and bottom right, 54 left.
Ideal Standard: 72 left, 72-73, 73 top right, 76, 77 bottom right, 78 bottom left and bottom right, 82 top right.
Ikea Ltd: 71 top right and bottom.
Marston & Langinger: 50 left and right, 51 top right.
Next Interiors: 11 bottom, 13 top left and bottom left, 29 bottom left, 39 bottom right, 40 top left, 48 right, 51 bottom right, 52 bottom left, 53 bottom right, 56 right, 57 top right and bottom, 61 top left, centre and bottom right, 66 left and right, 69 top left, top right and bottom right, 70 left, 78 top left, 85 top, right of centre, 86 bottom right, 87 right, 93 bottom right.
Taylor Alden /Alno (UK) Limited: 6 left of centre, 42 bottom, 43 left, top right, right of centre and bottom right, 44 bottom, 74 top left, 85 bottom left.
Touchstone: 6-7 bottom, 16 top left, 42 top, 44 top, 45 top right, right of centre and bottom right, 60 bottom left, 61 top right, 64 bottom left.
Welbeck Golin/Harris Communications Ltd: **Dulux** 7 bottom right, 15 left, 17 top left, bottom left, below centre, top right and right of centre, 23 right, 24, 25 top, 26-27, 27 top right and right of centre, 32-33, 33 top left, top right and bottom left, 40 right, 45 top left, 46, 47 above centre, top right, centre and bottom right, 56 left, 57 top left, 58 bottom left, below centre and bottom right, 62 left, centre and right, 63, 82 bottom right.

INDEX